READING INVENTORY
FOR THE CLASSROOM

FIFTH EDITION

E. Sutton Flynt
Austin Peay State University

Robert B. Cooter, Jr.
University of Texas at Arlington

Illustrations by Deborah S. Flynt

PEARSON

Merrill
Prentice Hall

Upper Saddle River, New Jersey
Columbus, Ohio

Library of Congress Cataloging-in-Publication Data

Flynt, E. Sutton
  Flynt-Cooter reading inventory for the classroom / E. Sutton
 Flynt, Robert B. Cooter, Jr.; illustrations by Deborah S. Flynt.—5th ed.
    Reading inventory for the classroom
      p. cm.
    Includes bibliographical references.
    ISBN 0-13-112106-5 (pbk.:alk. paper)
    1. Reading–Ability testing. 2. Reading comprehension–Ability testing.

LB1050.46 .F59 2004
428.4/076 21

                              2003044487

Vice President and Executive Publisher: Jeffery W. Johnston
Senior Editor: Linda Ashe Montgomery
Editorial Assistant: Laura Weaver
Production Editor: Mary M. Irvin
Production Coordinator: Carlisle Publishers Services
Design Coordinator: Diane C. Lorenzo
Cover Designer: Ali Mohrman
Cover Image: Christy Terry
Production Manager: Pamela D. Bennett
Director of Marketing: Ann Castel Davis
Marketing Manager: Darcy Betts Prybella
Marketing Coordinator: Tyra Poole

This book was set in Galliard by Carlisle Communications, Ltd. It was printed and bound by Courier Kendallville, Inc. The cover was printed by The Lehigh Press, Inc.

Pearson Education Ltd.
Pearson Education Singapore Pte. Ltd.
Pearson Education Canada, Ltd.
Pearson Education—Japan

Pearson Education Australia Pty. Limited
Pearson Education North Asia Ltd.
Pearson Educación de Mexico, S.A. de C.V.
Pearson Education Malaysia Pte. Ltd.

PEARSON
Merrill
Prentice Hall

10 9 8 7 6 5 4 3 2 1
ISBN: 0-13-112106-5

ACKNOWLEDGMENTS

Reading Inventory for the Classroom (*RIC*) was developed and revised to provide inservice and preservice teachers with a simple, straightforward means of assessing student reading development. The following individuals and groups provided a great deal of assistance during the development and revision of the inventory. As a result of their insights and suggestions, the *RIC* is a better, more effective inventory for use with children and adolescents. We would like to extend our appreciation to the teachers of Dallas Public Schools and to the reviewers of the manuscript: Kathleen Spencer Cooter, Texas Christian University, and to Rhea A. Ashmore, the University of Montana; Elaine V. Batenhorst, the University of Nebraska–Kearney; Tim Campbell, University of Central Oklahoma; Paula S. Currie, Southeastern Louisiana University; Susie Emond, Saginaw Valley State University; Kathy Escamilla, University of Colorado, Denver; Marguerite K. Gillis, Southwest Texas State University; and Maria J. Meyerson, the University of Nevada–Las Vegas; we appreciate their comments and insights.

Also, thanks to Claudia Cornett, Wittenberg University; Shirley Freed, Andrews University; Carolyn M. Griffin, Mabee Reading Clinic; Victoria J. Risko, Vanderbilt University; D. Ray Reutzel, Southern Utah University; Linda Gambrell, University of Maryland; Mary Lou Curley, San Antonio Independent School District; Patrice Werner, Southwest Texas State University; Bill King, Westside Elementary School; the Chapter I Teachers, San Antonio Independent School District; the faculty and students at Westside Elementary School; and the faculty and students at George Nettels Elementary School. Special thanks to John Lidh and Laser Precision for the use of Information and OTDRs.

Thanks to the reviewers of our manuscript for their suggestions and comments: Diane Bottomley, Ball State University; Laurie English-Piper, Northern Illinois University; Cyndi Giorgis, University of Nevada Las Vegas; Betty Goerss, Indiana University East; and Elizabeth D. Heins, Stetson University.

E. Sutton Flynt
Robert B. Cooter, Jr.

CONTENTS

FORM C

FORM D

Form *E*

■ ■ ■ ■ ■ ■ ■ ■ ■

INTRODUCTION

A spirited dialogue has been taking place for many years among reading educators regarding the role and nature of reading assessment. Valencia and Pearson (1987) captured an important point of consensus in the debate with the following statement:

> What we need are not just new and better tests. We need a new framework for thinking about assessment, one in which educators begin by considering types of decisions needed and the level of impact of those decisions. (p. 729)

The need for practitioners to use assessment instruments like the *Reading Inventory for the Classroom* (*RIC*) heightened in 2001 when Congress passed the *No Child Left Behind Act* (NCLB Act). The purpose of the NCLB Act is to close the achievement gap between disadvantaged students and their peers. Special emphasis has been placed on grades 1–3 via a section of the Act entitled *Reading First*. *Reading First* encourages training in administering screening, diagnostic, and classroom-based instructional assessments. We have attempted to design the new **Reading Inventory for the Classroom,** 5th edition to assist teachers in meeting the goals of the NCLB Act of identifying students who may be at risk of reading failure and planning interventions for those students.

Several important questions posed by teachers helped guide the construction of this instrument. One common questions was: *What decisions are required of classroom teachers, specialists, and clinicians in the initial assessment of students' reading development?* To answer this question, you should first think about your own perspective on teaching and learning. Our beliefs are drawn from what is known as *transactional theory* (Rosenblatt, 1978). Reutzel and Cooter (2004), in discussing transactional theory, explained that when someone reads, the reader's own knowledge and memories influence how the text is understood. Their *reasons* for reading (what transactional theorists call "social-situational context") likewise have an impact on how the reader performs. We also believe that evidence-based reading research proves that students need balanced or "comprehensive" reading instruction—a combination of explicit skill instruction within the context of enticing reading selections and writing instruction (Fountas & Pinnell, 1996, 1999, 2000; Holdaway, 1979; Reutzel, 1999; Reutzel & Cooter, 2003, 2004).

We feel that reading assessment should offer the teacher insights into students' literacy development, background knowledge, and the types of text students may have difficulty reading. This perspective contrasts sharply with more traditional views of reading assessment that tend to focus exclusively on the testing of discrete subskills with little or no attention to affective or social-situational contexts.

We note that, at present, many teachers may still be in a "transitional" phase of teaching (Reutzel & Cooter, 2004), moving gradually toward balanced reading instruction while still using many traditional materials and practices. This reading inventory, therefore, retains some traditional methods and descriptions that are easily identifiable to teachers in an early stage of transition, as well as balanced reading methods (Reutzel & Cooter, 2004) that are more consistent with current thinking about assessment.

The kinds of teaching and intervention decisions possible with the *Reading Inventory for the Classroom (RIC)* relate to such areas as:

- initial assessment of students' prereading capabilities
- phonemic awareness, alphabetic principle, and phonics knowledge
- students' use of decoding strategies
- structural analysis (root words, prefixes, suffixes)
- onset and rime
- aspects of reading print (selected words, punctuation, fluency)
- attention to story elements and content text elements
- literal, inferential, and evaluative comprehension abilities
- reading fluency and fluency reading rate

From these and other data derived from the inventory, teachers can begin to make decisions related to the kinds of reading skills to be addressed during instruction, materials that can be used effectively, the pacing of instruction, and the proper emphases of guided instruction (Fountas & Pinnell, 1996, 1999, 2001). Data gathered using the *RIC* should, of course, be viewed only as one part of a comprehensive assessment. Results can be used as part of students' reading portfolios, for determining first steps in teaching, or as evidence to be shared in meetings with family members and other professionals that focus on whether students should receive special services.

Another question for teachers that naturally follows is: *What is the level of impact of these decisions?* This question could have many interpretations based on the teacher's assignment. For the classroom reading teacher, the level of impact usually relates to the matching of instructional methods and materials to the student's point of development in reading and what they are ready to learn next with the aid of a skilled reading teacher/coach—what Vygotsky (1962) referred to as the student's *zone of proximal development.*

WHAT IS THE *FLYNT-COOTER READING INVENTORY FOR THE CLASSROOM?*

The *RIC* is an informal reading inventory intended for reading levels from preprimer through grade 12. It was developed to meet the needs of professionals interested in assessing the reading competencies of students in public or private schools, intervention programs, or clinical settings. The primary purpose of the inventory is to assist teachers in the preliminary placement of students with appropriate reading and instructional materials. Additionally, the inventory can be used for educating preservice and inservice teachers enrolled in college courses pertaining to reading assessment and the analysis of results. Finally, because the *RIC* has several equivalent versions, or "forms," it can be used as a posttest at mid-year or other times to determine the extent to which instruction has been successful since the first testing (pretest) was administered.

DESCRIPTION OF THE *FLYNT-COOTER RIC*

The inventory begins with an Interest/Attitude Interview designed to assist the examiner in establishing rapport with the student and to gather information about socially relevant factors that may be influencing the student's reading habits. It can also aid in the selection of topics and materials for use in classroom and remedial settings. Both a primary-level interview and an upper-level interview are provided in the Appendix.

The assessment portion of the inventory is divided into five forms: A, B, C, D, and E. Each of Forms A, B, C, and D includes three sections: sentences to determine the initial starting point for students (i.e., passage selection), the reading passages, and matching assessment protocols for the examiner's use. Form E has no accompanying sentences for initial passage selection because it is used only with students who read at upper high school levels.

In Forms A, B, C, and D, the section entitled "Sentences for Initial Passage Selection" is a series of sentences designed to help examiners choose the student's first reading passage, which ranges from Level 1 through Level 9. (*Note:* Special instructions are provided later for administering the preprimer assessment to students who do not perform well on Level 1 sentences.)

We use leveled sentences, rather than the graded word lists commonly used in informal reading inventories, because reading words in sentences is much closer to normal reading than reading words in isolation. The words used in Form A sentences are drawn in part from the Form A narrative passages, as is true for Forms B, C, and D. Therefore, if an examiner is going to use Form A, he or she should use sentences in Form A to determine the starting point for reading the passages.

The reading selections were written or adapted by the authors. Topics for the passages were selected based on our interviews with numerous school-age students with whom we have worked over the years as well as with our own children.

The *RIC* includes Levels PP and P (Preprimer and Primer) in Forms A and B. Special instructions for administering these passages are provided in the next section. All passages are leveled such that Level PP corresponds to beginning first-grade reading difficulty and Level 12 corresponds to 12th-grade difficulty. Forms A and B are narrative (story) passages, while Forms C, D, and E are expository (factual/content-oriented) passages. Passage difficulty was determined using a combination of widely respected procedures, including the Fry Readability Graph (1968) and the Harris-Jacobson Readability Formula (1975). All passages are within the assigned ranges.

Following the reading selections in each of the forms are *examiner's protocol forms* for analysis of student reading ability. The protocols include an introductory prereading statement, comprehension questions, a newly revised miscue analysis grid, a new section for analyzing results and determining whether to continue testing, and a listening comprehension assessment. For narrative passages, each of the comprehension questions is labeled according to story grammar element and hierarchical levels (literal, inferential, evaluative) of comprehension. For expository passages, each question is labeled by a designation we refer to as *expository grammar element* (based on the work of Meyer & Freedle, 1984) and traditional levels of comprehension.

A unique feature of the *RIC* is the inclusion of a new miscue grid for each passage. These grids, once completed by the examiner, will assist examiners in identifying error patterns made by students that can, in turn, lead to teaching decisions. A chart is provided at the end of each protocol to assist in determining whether to continue the assessment.

A new addition to the 5th edition of the *RIC* is a protocol for assessing students' reading fluency rate. This addition requires the examiner to time each passage the student is asked to ready orally. The procedure for using these protocols is discussed more fully in the next section. A scored student example is provided on pages 25–32.

How well does the *Flynt/Cooter Reading Inventory for the Classroom*, 5th Edition, align with the findings of the National Reading Panel?

In 1997, the United States Congress asked the director of the National Institute of Child Health and Human Development (NICHD) and the Secretary of Education to convene a national panel to assess the status of research-based knowledge on reading instruction. This National Reading Panel, as it came to be known, issued its report in April 2000.

Included in this *Report of the National Reading Panel* was a call for improved classroom instruction in several key areas: *alphabetics* (phonemic awareness and phonics instruction), *fluency* (reading rate, accuracy, and intonation), *vocabulary knowledge*, and *text comprehension*. The panel made it clear that effective teachers (1) understand how reading develops in each of these critical areas, (2) have the ability to quickly and efficiently assess each of their students to learn which skills are already known and which are still developing, and (3) can use assessment information to plan instruction targeting student needs.

The *Flynt/Cooter Reading Inventory for the Classroom*, 5th edition, has been designed to assist teachers in performing this second essential task—quickly and efficiently assessing each student's reading ability to learn which skills are already known and which are still developing. Specifically, you will be able to learn a great deal about student reading development in the following areas:

- *Alphabetics*—The Oral Reading and Analysis of Miscues sections enable you to analyze the student's use of basic phonics skills and syntax.

- *Fluency*—Included in this edition are charts and a procedure to assist you in determining the reading fluency rate of students.

- *Vocabulary knowledge*—In the sections titled Silent Reading Comprehension and Oral Reading and Analysis of Miscues, you will be able to learn a good deal about the student's specific knowledge of key words appearing in text.

- *Text comprehension*—The sections titled Silent Reading Comprehension specifically target this all-important skill. Further, you will be able to compare the student's ability to comprehend both fiction and nonfiction texts by using the parallel forms provided.

HOW DO *FLYNT-COOTER RIC* READING LEVELS COMPARE TO *GUIDED READING* LEVELS?

Teachers who use *Guided Reading* (Fountas & Pinnell, 1996, 1999, 2001) strategies frequently ask how reading level designations for the reading passages in the *RIC* compare to *Guided Reading* levels. Or, more to the point, can the *RIC* levels be translated into *Guided Reading* levels? This can be done easily using Table 1, which provides approximate translations. Levels will vary somewhat between passages, of course, but these translations will provide useful beginning points for selecting leveled literature from *Guided Reading* book collections to use in instructional lessons.

Also included is a translation of the *RIC* passages to levels commonly used in *Reading Recovery* and other similar one-to-one tutorial leveling systems. In the final column we provide yet another comparison—approximate stages of reading development. *Guided Reading* levels are included in each protocol along with the traditional grade level designation for each passage.

COMPARING THE *FLYNT-COOTER RIC* READING LEVELS AND *GUIDED READING* LEVELS (FOUNTAS & PINNELL, 1999, 2001) A–Z

Reutzel and Cooter (2003, pp. 64–67, 113) developed a text gradient summary by grade level of *Guided Reading* criteria for determining Emergent Literacy through the Intermediate grades, reading levels (A–Z). We have adapted it to include correlations with passages from the *Reading Inventory for the Classroom*.

TABLE 1 Reading Level Translations: *Flynt-Cooter RIC* (5th ed.) to *Guided Reading* to *One-to-One Tutoring* to *Stages of Reading Development*

READING LEVEL TRANSLATIONS

Flynt-Cooter RIC Reading Level	*Guided Reading* Level (Fountas-Pinnell, 1996)	*One-to-One Tutoring* Level (e.g., *Reading Recovery*, etc.)	Approx. Stages of Reading Development
RIC: Preschool–Kindergarten*			Emergent
RIC: PP (Preprimer)	A B	1 2	Emergent
RIC: P (Primer)	C D E	3 4 6–8	Early
RIC: Level 1	F G H I	10 12 14 16	Early / Transitional
RIC: Level 2	J–K L–M	18–20 24–28	Transitional
RIC: Level 3	N O–P	30 34–38	Transitional / Fluent/Extending
RIC: Level 4	Q–R	40	Fluent/Extending
RIC: Level 5	Not applicable	44	Fluent/Extending
RIC: Level 6 and above	Not applicable	Not applicable	Fluent/Extending

*Preschool–Kindergarten is not one of the *Flynt-Cooter RIC* (5th ed.) reading levels. However, students may well attain preprimer and higher levels in kindergarten.

RIC Preprimer (PP) through *RIC* Primer (P) Level: *Guided Reading* Levels A–D (Fountas & Pinnell, 1999)

- Language patterns are repeated.
- Illustrations match and explain most of the text. Actions are clearly presented without much in the way of extraneous detail that might confuse the reader.
- The whole meaning or story is likely to match the experiences and conceptual knowledge common to most beginning readers.
- The language of the text developmentally matches syntax and organization of most young children's speech for which the text is intended.
- Sentences and books themselves are comparatively short (10–60 words).
- Print is carefully laid out so that it appears consistently in the same place on the page throughout each book.
- By Level D sentences are longer and more words with inflected endings are present.
- Pictures continue to be important, but the story is carried by the print by Level C.

Assumption at this level: When students encounter an unknown word in print, they can easily use context from known words and illustrations along with language pattern cues and early word analysis skills for successful decoding.

RIC Primer (P): *Guided Reading* Levels D–E (Fountas & Pinnell, 1999)

- One often sees predictable, repetitive language patterns, but the same pattern does not dominate the entire text.
- Language patterns are more varied, as opposed to one or two word changes, for example.
- Words and phrases may appear to express different meanings through varying sentence structures.
- By the end of these stages, the syntax is more typical of written or "book" language.
- Illustrations provide minimal support for readers determining exact language.
- Word analysis skills are increasingly required.

RIC Primer (P) through *RIC* Level 1: *Guided Reading* Levels E–G (Fountas & Pinnell, 1999)

- Variation in sentence patterns is now the norm.
- Sentences are longer with less predictable text and repetition.
- Written language styles and genre become more prominent, including the use of some verb forms not often used by young children in oral settings.
- The average sentence length in texts increases.
- Events in a story may continue over several pages. They have a definite beginning, middle, and end.
- Concepts may be less familiar to students.
- Use of dialogue increases.
- Illustrations provide only moderate support to the meaning of the stories.

RIC Level 1: *Guided Reading* Levels G–I (Fountas & Pinnell, 1999)

- There is a greater variety of words and the inclusion of more specialized vocabulary.
- Like Level F, pictures provide some support for the overall meaning of the story, but cannot be used by the reader to interpret the precise message.
- Stories are longer.

RIC Level 2: *Guided Reading* Levels J–M (Fountas & Pinnell, 1999)

- There are now longer stories or sequences of events.
- Story events are developed more fully than those in texts at lower levels.
- Vocabulary is progressively more rich and varied.

- Illustrations are used to help to create the atmosphere and setting, rather than to specifically depict the content of the text.
- It is now common to have full pages of print with no illustrations.
- Point of view is introduced.
- Chapter books appear during these levels.
- Texts are more varied and include information texts.

RIC Level 3: *Guided Reading* Levels N–P (Fountas & Pinnell, 1999)

- More emphasis is placed on reading informational texts.
- A single plot is typically presented.
- Length of books expands and word analysis is required.
- Many new multisyllable words are used in these texts.
- A variety of genres appear, requiring greater ability to interpret new meanings.

RIC Level 4: *Guided Reading* Levels Q–S (Fountas & Pinnell, 2001)

- Sentences are more complex and vocabulary more difficult.
- Complexity of plot and themes increase.
- Multiple points of view are presented.
- Very few illustrations appear at this level.

RIC Level 5: *Guided Reading* Levels T–V (Fountas & Pinnell, 2001)

- Symbolism is used by authors at these levels.
- Genres include fantasy, historical fiction, and realistic fiction.
- Informational texts contain technical information in graphic displays.
- Print is smaller.
- Narratives contain multiple plot lines and subplots.

RIC Level 6: *Guided Reading* Levels W–Z* (Fountas & Pinnell, 2001)

(*Consider these levels to extend beyond Level 6 of the *RIC*.)

- Books become more complex and sophisticated.
- Literary devices are used that go beyond the literal level.
- Science fiction presents more technical information.
- Information books address social and political issues.

WHO SHOULD USE THE *FLYNT-COOTER RIC*?

The *RIC* is appropriate for preservice teachers (i.e., college students enrolled in teacher education programs), inservice teachers, and other education professionals involved with students who have reading needs. It provides valuable insights into reading development, especially word identification, story and content comprehension, and reading fluency. Classroom teachers who use basal reading programs will find the inventory quite useful for placement decisions.

Teachers who use literature-based reading programs will find the inventory helpful in planning collaborative learning activities that involve reading, planning mini-lessons, and determining which nonnegotiable reading skills (Reutzel & Cooter, 2004) need further development. The *RIC* can also provide a valuable starting place for portfolio assessment profiles. In an intervention or clinical education setting, it can be used as part of an assessment training program as well as an investigative tool for research purposes.

HOW THE *FLYNT-COOTER RIC* DIFFERS FROM OTHER INFORMAL READING INVENTORIES

From the outset, we wanted to create an easy-to-use inventory—one that focuses on identifying student strengths, helps teachers plan for instruction, and reflects the current state of knowledge concerning the assessment of reading processes. We also wanted to develop an instrument that is traditional in appearance and may be used by reading educators who have a more traditional view of reading education. The 5th edition of the *RIC* has a number of features that help satisfy these goals:

- *Emergent reader rubric*—The *RIC* contains a unique method for assessing prereading capabilities using balanced reading assessment procedures. These rubrics are found in the examiner's protocols for the Preprimer (PP) and Primer (P) levels.

- *Miscue grids*—Informed instruction is based on repeating patterns of behavior, not one-time errors in oral reading. Each passage protocol includes a miscue analysis grid containing a facsimile of the passage, space for marking oral reading miscues, analysis columns, and space for tallying the numbers and types of miscues. These grids make quick and accurate assessment of error patterns possible and assist the teacher in planning intervention sessions based on student need.

- *Miscue analysis form*—Following each miscue grid is a new miscue analysis form. It will help you to identify specific reading skills and strategies the student needs to develop.

- *Interest/Attitude Interview*—Interest, attitude, and motivation are critical factors to consider when planning instruction. This *RIC* subtest is designed to gather affective information about students.

- *High-interest passages*—Students demonstrate their best reading abilities when reading passages that interest them. The passages in this inventory reflect some of the prominent interests of students in elementary and secondary school settings.

- *Longer passages*—Passages are longer in the *RIC* than those in other informal reading inventories. This allows for full development of story information and context and creates more authentic ("real reading") situations to be observed.

- *Correlation of reading passage levels with* Guided Reading *(Fountas & Pinnell, 1996, 1999, 2001) and* Reading Recovery *levels*—As seen earlier in this book, a chart is provided for easy conversions of our passages with *Guided Reading* books as well as inclusion of how these determinations are made to assist you with other passages and books. Approximate conversions for *RIC* passages with *Reading Recovery* materials is also presented in Table 1.

- *Passage retellings*—Sometimes students can feel that the excessive comprehension questioning following the reading of a passage is like an interrogation. Asking students to retell the critical points of a passage, according to research, is a more authentic and informative approach to assessment and is also much less stressful for students. Retellings are used at all levels of this inventory; hence, only questions that relate to text information not recounted by the student are asked, making comprehension assessment quicker and more comprehensive.

- *Story grammar analyses*—Carefully researched views of reading comprehension confirm the effectiveness of the story grammar perspective (e.g., setting, characterization, story problem, resolution, theme). Each question in the silent reading/retelling section of Forms A and B (narrative selections) is keyed to story grammar categories and to traditional hierarchical labels (literal, inferential, and evaluative).

- *Expository text grammars*—Just as narrative passages are keyed to the story grammar perspective, expository selections in Forms C and D are keyed to text types (expository text grammars) based on the work of Meyer and Freedle (1984) and to traditional comprehension labels.

- *Reading fluency rate*—The importance of assessing a student's reading fluency rate has led us to include a method for determining this aspect of reading growth. Assessing a student's reading fluency rate is important because it indicates whether a student is focusing more on word recognition or comprehension.

- *Intervention strategies*—Once error patterns are determined, a partial listing of possible instructional interventions is suggested. These examples are offered to illustrate what we refer to as *If → Then Thinking* (ways of analyzing assessment data and forming instructional decisions). This procedure is included in the following section.

Administration and Scoring Procedures

STEP 1: INTEREST/ATTITUDE INTERVIEW

One of the most important, and often ignored, aspects of reading assessment is the affective domain. Affect involves interest, attitude, and motivational factors related to reading success. We include an Interest/Attitude Interview to assist examiners in learning more about students' background knowledge, interests, and motivations that may relate to reading success. Information from this brief survey should be used in the selection of reading materials that will be appealing to the student.

Two versions of the Interest/Attitude Interview are included: Primary Form and Upper Level Form. The Primary Form is intended for students in grades 1 and 2, and the Upper Level Form is intended for grades 3 through 12. In each case, the examiner begins with the introductory statement provided on the form, then proceeds by asking each of the questions. (See Appendix, pp. 313–344.) It is the intention of the authors that examiners use these questions as a springboard for discussion, not simply as a rote exercise. Similarly, examiners should feel free to disregard any questions they feel are inappropriate.

Research on the affective domain and how it relates to reading success is rather sparse, and recommendations for using data derived from an interview of this sort are few. However, most teacher-examiners find that information derived from the Interest/Attitude Interview can be beneficial in several ways. First, information about reading interests can help the teacher to select reading materials that are appealing to students and, therefore, choose texts matched to students' background knowledge and vocabulary. Second, information derived from questions related to reading and study habits at home can provide teachers with insights and appropriate suggestions for parents. Third, students often help teachers understand what their strengths and needs are in reading through the students' answers to such questions as "What makes a person a good reader?" and "What causes a person to not be a good reader?" The Interest/Attitude Interview will not tell teachers everything they need to know about students' abilities, but it *will* help in finding an informed departure point for quality reading experiences.

STEP 2: SENTENCES FOR INITIAL PASSAGE SELECTION

Begin by having students read the set of placement sentences at the beginning of the selected form of the inventory (Forms A, B, C, and D). We suggest having students begin reading sentences two grade levels below their current grade placement, if possible. This will help avoid potential student frustration caused by starting with passages that are too difficult. If the student is in grades 1, 2, or 3, begin with Level 1 sentences. (*Note:* If students do not perform well on the Level 1 sentences, see the instructions on pages 20–22 for administering the Preprimer and Primer passages.) **Have students continue reading sets of placement sentences until they miss two words or more, then stop. The highest level of** placement sentences read with zero errors should be the level of the first passage to be read by the student.

(Note: We often find it is best to start students two full levels below where they first missed two or more words. For example, if the student first misses two or more words at Level 5, then it may be best to have the student begin reading at Level 3. This avoids inadvertently starting students at their frustration level.)

For students who have no error through Level 9, begin with Form E, Level 10.

STEP 3: READING PASSAGES

As mentioned previously, students should begin reading the passage indicated by their performance on the initial passage selection sentences. Examiners should place in front of the student a copy of the passage from which the student will read. In schools where a great deal of assessment takes place, we recommend that the student copies be laminated.

Examiners should turn to the corresponding protocol form for that passage and follow along. **Permission is granted to teachers purchasing the *RIC* to duplicate these protocol forms for their own classroom needs.** Note that each protocol is divided into Parts I, II, III, and IV. A step-by-step description is offered for each section.

Part I: Silent Reading Comprehension

1. Read the background statement aloud and say that you will ask for a retelling of the passage after the student has read it silently. Then allow the student to read the passage once silently.

2. After the silent reading is completed, remove the passage and ask the student to retell what he or she remembers about the passage. Check off each question in Part I that is answered during the student's retelling by placing "ua" in the appropriate blank to indicate the student was *unaided*. Ask all of the remaining questions not covered in the student's retelling or that need clarification. Place "a" in the appropriate blank next to each question that the student answers correctly to indicate the student was *aided* in recalling this information.

3. Because of the level of reading sophistication of students above the ninth grade, we recommend that students who are asked to read the passages at levels 10, 11, and 12 in Form E only read the passage silently. We feel it is unnecessary at these levels to assess students' oral reading behaviors. However, for those who wish to conduct oral reading at these levels, a grid has been provided.

Part II: Oral Reading and Analysis of Miscues

Next, have the student read the passage orally up to the *oral reading stop-marker (///)* noted on the miscue grid (see the example on page 27). Note any miscues on the passage facsimile portion of the grid. A description of miscues and how to mark them on the grid is included in the next section. It is based on the work of Clay (1985), Fountas and Pinnell (1996), and Reutzel and Cooter (2004). Note that the grid should *not* be completed during the oral reading (completion is probably not possible in any case), but should be completed *after* the assessment session has been concluded with the student. Oral reading miscues should be noted on the passage facsimile as the student is reading. We recommend that the student's voice also be tape-recorded during the retelling and oral reading to allow for convenient review at a later time and to establish permanent audio records of the child's reading development. As noted, miscue grids should be completed after the assessment session with the child has been concluded.

Miscue Grid: "ERROR TYPE"

- *Mispronunciation*

Student incorrectly pronounces a word. Mispronunciations typically are nonwords. Write the incorrect pronunciation above the word on the protocol.

Student: "*The* deg *ran away*"

Notation: The d̶o̶g̶ ran away. *(deg written above dog)*

- *Substitution*

Student substitutes a real word or words for a word in the text. Draw a line through the word and write what the student said above it.

Student: "*The* tree *was very high.*"

Notation: The c̶l̶o̶u̶d̶ was very high. *(tree written above cloud)*

- *Insertion*

A word is added that is *not* in the text. An insertion symbol (∧) is recorded between the two appropriate words, and the inserted word is written above the insertion symbol.

Student: "*He'll want to have a look in the mirror.*"

Notation: He'll want to ∧ look in the mirror. *(have a written above insertion symbol)*

- *Teacher assistance*

The student is "stuck" on a word and the teacher pronounces it. Record the incident as "TA" (teacher-assisted). This error is also counted when the student asks for help during silent reading.

Notation: autom(TA)obile *(TA circled above automobile)*

- *Repetition*

The student repeats a word or series of words. A repetition is recorded by underlining the word(s) that are repeated. This category is recorded as additional observational data but *does not* figure in the determination of whether to continue testing or not. Therefore, in determining the number of miscues a student makes on a passage, repetitions are not a part of the final tally.

Student: "*The boy wanted to wanted to go to the show.*"

Notation: The boy <u>wanted to</u> go to the show.

- *Omission*

If no word (or words) is given, the error is noted by circling the word(s) omitted on the protocol.

Notation: The cloud was (very) high.

- *Error totals*

At this point in using the miscue grid, indicate the total of miscues for each line of text. You can cross-check the error total by totaling each vertical column corresponding to each error type. By totaling each vertical column, it is possible to determine which miscue type the student is making repeatedly. Note that self-corrections (described next) are not counted as miscues.

- *Self-correction*

The student corrects a miscue himself. Self-corrections are noted by writing "SC," but should not be counted as errors in the final tally, unless the student never correctly pronounces the word.

Student: "*The money . . . the monkey was funny.*"

Notation: "The monkey was funny."

Miscue Grid: "ERROR ANALYSIS"—Meaning, Syntax, and Visual Cues (MSV)

The 5th edition of the *Reading Inventory for the Classroom* includes several new points of analysis on the miscue grid. With these tools patterned after procedures perfected by Clay (1985) in her widely acclaimed *Reading Recovery* program, you will be able to determine to what extent three strategies are being used when a miscue occurs: meaning (M), syntax (S), and visual cues (V). A brief explanation of each follows:

- *M = Semantic (Meaning—Does it make sense?)*

In reviewing each miscue, consider whether the student is using meaning cues in his or her attempt to identify the word. Context clues, picture cues, or information from the passage are possible examples of meaning cues used by the reader.

- *S = Structure (Syntax—Does it sound right?)*

A rule system, or grammar, as with all languages, governs the English language. For example, English is essentially based on a "subject-verb" grammar system. *Syntax* is the application of this subject-verb grammar system in creating sentences. The goal in studying *syntax cues* as a part of your miscue analysis is to try to determine the extent to which the student unconsciously uses rules of grammar in attempting to identify unknown words in print. For example, if a word in a passage causing a miscue for the reader is a verb, ask yourself whether the student's miscue was also a verb. Consistent use of the appropriate part of speech in miscues (i.e., a noun for a noun, a verb for a verb, articles for articles, etc.) is an indication that the student has internalized the rule system of English grammar and is applying that knowledge in attacking unknown words.

- *V = Visual (Graphophonic—Does it look right?)*

Sometimes a miscue looks a good bit like the correct word appearing in the text. The miscue may begin with the same letter or letters; for example, saying *top* for *toy,* or *sit* for *seat*. Another possibility is the letters of the miscue may look very similar to the word appearing in text (e.g., *introduction* for *introspection*). The extent to which readers use visual cues is an important factor to consider when trying to better understand the skills employed by developing readers when attacking unknown words in print.

Part III: Miscue Analysis

In this section, the examiner takes a closer look at the student's reading miscues to determine his or her strengths and needs. Remember that a single miscue is not significant in and of itself. Instead, look for repeated miscues that form a pattern on which to base your instructional decisions. It will most likely require that you look for the same types of miscues over several passages in order to discover patterns. Brief definitions for each of the miscue types found in the Miscue Analysis segment for each passage follow.

A. Fundamental Behaviors Observed

This section will be relevant only for emergent and early readers (see Reutzel & Cooter, 2004, for a full description of developmental levels). Hence, you may wish to omit this section for students beginning at Level 3 or higher.

L → R Directionality—"Left to Right Directionality" refers to whether the student is reading properly from left to right on the page as well as from top to bottom.

1 to 1 Matching—"One to One Matching" is the ability to call the correct letter or word when reading or *tracking* across the page.

Searching for Clues—Looking for clues in the text to identify the unknown word (e.g., looking back for information, studying the picture).

Cross-Checking—Checking one clue against another.

B. Word Attack Behaviors

No Attempt—Does not attempt to pronounce the word.

Mispronunciation (Invented Word)—Reader says a nonsense or invented word in place of the actual word (e.g., *blonk* for *black, mitkow* for *motorcar*).

Substitutes—Calls out another word in place of the actual word in text (e.g., *motorcycle* for *motorcar, belt* for *bike, mountain* for *hill*, etc.). Note that substitutions may or may not begin with the same letter, and they may not be the correct part of speech (syntax).

Skips/Reads On—Skips an unknown word in print and reads on after first attempting to decode it.

Asks for Help—Asks the examiner for assistance when coming to an unknown word.

Repeats—Rereads a word or phrase in the text.

Attempts to Self-Correct—Recognizes that a miscue was made and tries to correct the error (either successfully or unsuccessfully).

"Sounds Out" (Segmenting)—Segments and pronounces unknown words in print phonetically, sound by sound using letter (grapheme) cues.

Blends Sounds—Blends sounds pronounced into a spoken word.

Structural Analysis (Root Words, Affixes)—Recognizes root words, prefixes, and/or suffixes in unknown words in print.

C. Cueing Systems Used in Attempting Words

Review the Error Analysis section beginning on page 14 for full descriptions of M, S, and V miscue types. The purpose of identifying miscue types is to assist you in collecting specific examples of each, along with the actual/correct words or phrases from the passage for comparisons. See Table 2 for more specific examples of miscues.

D. Fluency and Reading Fluency Rate (word by word → fluent reading)

As noted earlier, the examiner should record the number of seconds it takes the student to read each passage orally. These figures will be used to determine the student's oral reading fluency rate. In addition, the examiner should observe and record the student's oral reading behavior for each passage the student reads orally. The following descriptions, found on the protocol for each level of the *RIC,* provide the examiner some insight into how to rate the general fluency of the student.

TABLE 2 Selected Common Miscues and Intervention Strategies

Miscue Type	Examples from the *Flynt-Cooter RIC*	Problem Description	Possible Interventions
Mispronunciations (or possibly a substitution) **of Ending Sounds**	**Text:** *familiar* **Student reads as:** *family* or *famsom*	Student is decoding the first and middle part of the word, but not the ending.	If the student calls the word another word that doesn't make sense, then he is not using context clues. We suggest using story frames, discussion webs, or cloze/maze passages to emphasize the role of context in word identification (see Reutzel & Cooter, 2003).
Substitutions: Wrong Sounds	**Text:** *shoes* **Student reads as:** *feet*	Student reads as another word that fits the context, but not the correct word/letter sounds.	In this case, the student is ready to learn the basic word identification strategy (Reutzel & Cooter, 2003): Context Clues + beginning sound(s) + medial sounds. Using enlarged text with stick-on notes revealing only the word parts you wish to emphasize (e.g., beginning sound) is a great way to model and practice.
Mispronunciations: No Use of Context	**Text:** *through* **Student reads as:** *primly*	Student is making up nonsense words without regard to the context of the passage.	This indicates that the student may not realize that reading is a meaning-based language activity. Cooter & Flynt (1996) recommend the guided listening procedure and lookback organizers. These strategies are equally useful with expository reading.
Self-Corrections	**Text:** *loved* **Student reads as:** *lived, loved*	Student miscues on a word, then spontaneously self-corrects.	Self-corrections do not usually require intervention, but rather praise for reading strategically.
Insertions	**Text:** *Others who couldn't* . . . **Student reads as:** *Others who really couldn't* . . .	Student inserts words not actually in the text—a problem related to reading fluency.	Reutzel & Cooter (2003) recommend repeated readings, dialogue retellings, and student dramas as strategies that have students focus on accuracy.
Teacher Assists	**Text:** *any text* **Student reads as:** *No response from student*	Teacher must say word(s) for the student.	Teachers should supply unknown words after about 5 seconds to preserve student's short-term memory of the sentence. If this happens frequently, then the passage may be too difficult or the student may not have learned the word identification strategy mentioned previously.
Omissions	**Text:** *Some like ice cream, while others prefer soda.* **Student reads as:** *Some like ice cream, others prefer soda.*	Student leaves out a word(s) in the text.	This is usually a minor problem with accuracy or reading— a fluency type of miscue. See "Insertions" mentioned previously for fluency strategies. (Note: Sometimes omissions are the result of a regional or cultural dialect.)

Word by Word—Reads in a slow, labored, word-by-word fashion. Fairly long pauses between words, may exhibit little awareness of syntax, and/or decoding is obviously difficult.

Mixed Phrasing—A mixture of some word-by-word reading and reading fluently in one- or two-word phrases. May show attention to syntax and punctuation. Decoding is sometimes automatic and other times more labored. Punctuation is often ignored.

Fluent Reading—Reads mainly in fluent phrases with good expression. There is good attention to syntax and punctuation. Decoding seems to be automatic.

Reading Fluency Rate (Fluency Rate in Seconds)*—The reading fluency rate for each student is determined by:

1. recording the number of seconds it takes the student to read each passage orally and recording this figure on the fluency section of each passage's protocol. **(Please note that the reading fluency rate is based on the 100 words read orally and not the entire passage.)**

2. finding the average number of seconds required to complete the oral reading of all passages determined to be at the student's easy (independent) and adequate (instructional) reading level. (The examiner should add each passage's fluency rate and the number of seconds it took the student to read the passage and divide that number by the number of passages determined to be easy and adequate.)

3. using Table 3 to find the student's average number of seconds per 100 words.

TABLE 3   Reading Fluency Rate Conversion Chart

Average Number Seconds per 100 Words	Average Number Words per Minute			Average Number Seconds per 100 Words	Average Number Words per Minute
75	80			49	122
74	81			48	125
73	82			47	128
72	83			46	130
71	85			45	133
70	86			44	136
69	87			43	140
68	88			42	143
67	90			41	146
66	91			40	150
65	92			39	154
64	94			38	158
63	95			37	162
62	97			36	166
61	98			35	171

*Reading fluency rates are not appropriate for the Preprimer and Primer selections. Reading fluency rates for Form E requires a different approach. See Instructions for Administering Form E Passages on Page 22.

4. recording this figure on the Student Summary Form located in the Appendix.
5. using Table 4 to make a judgment about the student's reading fluency rate. (If a student's reading fluency rate is low in comparison to the established norms, then the examiner should consider this in determining instructional goals for the student.)

The Oral Reading Fluency (ORF) rates shown in Table 4 represent both minimum and maximum expectations for student in grades 1 through 5. The assumption is that students are reading at their instructional, or *adequate*, level.

As students enter grade 3, they should be helped to adapt their reading speed to fit the purpose and type of text. Readers should have a higher reading fluency rate when reading fictional stories (narrative) than when reading a nonfiction (expository) text.

Performance Summary

This final section helps examiners determine whether to continue testing and also explains how to identify the student's reading level. For Silent Reading Comprehension and Oral Reading Accuracy, a three-tier system is used. In each case, the examiner decides whether the passage appeared to be *easy, adequate,* or *too hard* for the student. These descriptors are based on the work of Powell (1969) and Betts (1946). **Easy** means that the passage can be read with few errors, and the student requires no additional assistance from others in similar texts. The easy level is comparable to the "independent" reading level designation used in traditional informal reading inventories. **Adequate** means that students can read the passage effectively but will likely require some help from another person to successfully comprehend the passage. The adequate level is comparable to the "instructional" reading level designation used in traditional informal reading inventories. **Too hard** means that the passage difficulty is sufficient to cause the reader much anxiety and frustration. This level is sometimes called the "frustration" reading level in traditional inventories.

Continue to the Next Reading Passage?

A student who scores at the *too hard* level in either Silent Reading Comprehension or Oral Reading Accuracy should not be administered the next higher level passage. Placement in reading materials should be at the level just below the passage

TABLE 4   Oral Reading Fluency End-Of-Year Goals for Grade Levels 1–5: Words per Minute (wpm)— Instructional Level (Adequate) Text

Grade Level	*Minimum* Words per Minute* (wpm)	Fluent Oral Reading (wpm)
Grade 1	60 wpm	80 wpm
Grade 2	70 wpm	100 wpm
Grade 3	80 wpm	126 wpm**
Grade 4	90 wpm	162 wpm**
Grade 5	100 wpm	180 wpm

*Adapted from the *Texas Essential Knowledge and Skills* (2001–2002). Texas Education Agency Website— http://www.tea.state.tx.us/

**Source: U.S. Department of Education, National Center for Education Statistics. *Listening to Children Read Aloud, 44.* Washington, DC: 1995.

receiving a *too hard* judgment. Thus, if a student first reaches a *too hard* score on Level 5 Silent Reading Comprehension, reading placement level for instructional purposes would be Level 4.

Part IV: Listening Comprehension (Reading "Potential")

Having students listen to a passage and then respond to questions about it is a traditional method used by some reading specialists to estimate a student's listening comprehension level or reading capacity. According to some authorities (Carroll, 1977; Durrell, 1969; Sinatra, 1990), establishing a student's listening comprehension level provides an indication of a student's reading capacity or potential at this stage of development. Reading capacity refers to the level a student has the potential of reaching if he or she receives appropriate reading experiences and instruction. The following details how one establishes a student's listening comprehension level using the *RIC.*

Once a student has reached the *too hard* (i.e., frustration) level on silent reading comprehension, you can establish the student's listening comprehension level. Begin by using the passage that is one level above the passage that reached the *too hard* level criteria for your student in silent reading. Tell the student that now you are going to read a story aloud. Encourage the student to listen carefully because you are going to ask some questions when you are finished reading. Using the background statement for the passage, read the passage out loud to the student. When you finish reading the passage, ask each of the questions provided for the passage. A student who can answer 75% or more of the questions has adequate listening comprehension. Continue reading higher level passages to the student until he or she falls below the 75% criterion. The highest level to which the student can respond to 75% of the questions correctly is considered to be that student's listening comprehension level. This level could also indicate the student's reading capacity. However, you should be cautioned that this information should be coupled with careful observation of the student in the testing session as well as his or her performance in the classroom.

STEP 4: COMPLETING THE STUDENT SUMMARY

Immediately following the scored student sample is a copy of the *RIC* Student Summary. Turn to Appendix p. 331 to find additional copies of the *RIC* Student Summary. These forms may be duplicated by examiners for classroom assessment use. Examiners should complete this summary after the assessment session(s) has been completed in order to gather information and begin to develop initial classroom intervention plans, should they be necessary. The *RIC* is only a starting point in the assessment and intervention process. We encourage teachers and examiners embarking on intervention programs to begin with what students know in order to continue sampling and gathering data about the student's reading abilities. This is what Marie Clay (1985) refers to as "roaming around the known." Clay suggests a two-week period of roaming around the known in her *Reading Recovery Programme*—the equivalent of about 5 hours spread over 2 weeks. This kind of continuing assessment, when used in conjunction with the *RIC,* yields rich descriptive information about the student. We feel this process should help the teacher and examiner learn more about the student's reading abilities, confirm or reject initial findings drawn from this inventory, and discover ways of helping students continue to grow as successful readers.

If → Then Analyses: Informing Your Teaching Using *Flynt-Cooter RIC* Data

After you have administered the *Reading Inventory for the Classroom* and completed the miscue grid and Miscue Analysis sections, you will begin to make some preliminary judgments about the student's instructional needs. (*Note:* It is important to remember to look for *patterns* of behavior, not isolated occurrences, as you consider options. Do not assume that because a student makes a certain kind of error once that it is in fact a problem for him or her.)

If → Then Thinking

One of the challenges facing teachers today is how to analyze assessment data and plan instruction that targets students' needs accurately. Success depends on three elements: (1) having a clear understanding of the stages of learning one goes through in becoming a fluent reader, (2) knowing how to assess students effectively to learn where they are in their learning development in reading, and (3) knowing how to apply research-proven best teaching practices in reading instruction according to student needs.

If→ Then Thinking is the essence of the third point just made. *If* you identify specific abilities and needs using the *RIC*, *then* what should you offer the student next in your teaching? Said another way, the teacher must first collect a good bit of information through classroom assessments that begins to paint a picture of where the student is in his or her reading development. Once that picture begins to take shape and the teacher has an educated impression of what the student is able to do independently in reading, then she should ask herself, "What is this student ready for in reading next? *If* the student can do these things independently in reading, *then* he is now ready to learn _____ ."

To provide some examples of how you can use miscue patterns as guides to informing your instruction using *If→ Then Thinking,* look back to Table 2. It describes a few common miscue patterns we have encountered with children, along with selected strategies described by Reutzel and Cooter (2004) in *Teaching Children to Read: Putting the Pieces Together* and Reutzel and Cooter's (2003) *Strategies for Reading Assessment and Instruction: Helping Every Child Succeed.* A list of these and other references that offer some of our favorite teaching strategies follows.

Recommended Books Containing Teaching Strategies

Cooter, R. B., & Flynt, E. S. (1996). *Teaching reading in the content areas: Developing content literacy for all students.* New York: John Wiley. ISBN 0-02-324711-8.

Fountas, I., & Pinnell, G. S. (1996). *Guided reading.* Portsmouth, NH: Heinemann. ISBN 0-435-08863-7.

Reutzel, D. R., & Cooter, R. B. (1999). *Balanced reading strategies and practices: Assessing and assisting readers with special needs.* Upper Saddle River, NJ: Merrill/Prentice Hall. ISBN 0-02-324715.

Reutzel, D. R., & Cooter, R. B. (2003). *Strategies for reading assessment and instruction: Helping every child succeed.* Upper Saddle River, NJ. Merrill/Prentice Hall.

Reutzel, D. R., & Cooter, R. B. (2004). *Teaching children to read: Putting the pieces together* (4 ed.). Upper Saddle River, NJ: Merrill/Prentice Hall. ISBN 0-13-099835-4.

INSTRUCTIONS FOR ADMINISTERING THE PREPRIMER (PP) AND PRIMER (P) PASSAGES

Passages for emergent readers in Forms A and B of the *RIC* have been given the conventional labels of Preprimer (PP) and Primer (P), but reflect a much more balanced view of early reading processes. We have drawn on recent research in emergent literacy (Adams, 1994; Clay, 1985; Morrow, 1993; Sulzby, 1985) to develop passages and procedures that can be used in beginning assessment in elementary classrooms. Although information gained from administering these passages can be useful to teachers early in the school year and for periodic assessments, we feel that regular student-teacher interactions using authentic storybooks are necessary for more complete assessment profiles.

In developing these passages, we have considered carefully the research of Cochrane and colleagues (1984) and Sulzby (1985), who have attempted to chronicle observable emergent reading developmental "milestones." To assist in the assessment of emergent readers, we have created checklists for the PP and P levels based on research findings in emergent literacy. The stages we have developed are:

Stage 1: Early Connections to Reading—Describing Pictures

- Attends to and describes (labels) pictures in books
- Has a limited sense of story
- Follows verbal directions for this activity
- Uses oral vocabulary appropriate for age/grade level
- Displays attention span appropriate for age/grade level
- Responds to questions in an appropriate manner
- Appears to connect pictures (sees them as being interrelated)

Stage 2: Connecting Pictures to Form a Story

- Attends to pictures and develops oral stories across the pages of the book
- Uses only childlike or descriptive (storyteller) language to tell the story, rather than book language (i.e., Once upon a time . . . ; There once was a little boy . . .)

Stage 3: Transitional Picture Reading

- Attends to pictures as a connected story
- Mixes storyteller language with book language

Stage 4: Advanced Picture Reading

- Attends to pictures and develops oral stories across the pages of the book
- Speaks as though reading the story (uses book language)

Stage 5: Early Print Reading

- Tells a story using the pictures
- Knows print moves from left to right, top to bottom
- Creates part of the text using book language and knows some words on sight

Stage 6: Early Strategic Reading

- Uses context to guess at some unknown words (guesses make sense)
- Notices beginning sounds in words and uses them in guessing unknown words
- Seems to sometimes use syntax to help identify words in print
- Recognizes some word parts, such as root words and affixes

Stage 7: Moderate Strategic Reading

- Sometimes uses context and word parts to decode words
- Self-corrects when making an oral reading miscue
- Retells the passage easily and may embellish the story line
- Shows some awareness of vowel sounds

In attempting to provide passages at emergent reading levels that correspond in some meaningful way with current knowledge of emergent literacy, we chose a simple but informative format. At the Preprimer (PP) level, we have provided a wordless picture book format for the narrative passages. In each case, the story is told using a series of four illustrations that tell a story when read or retold sequentially. This format will enable examiners to learn whether the student has progressed through the first three or four stages of emergent reading as just outlined. Passages at the Primer (P) level also use the four-illustration format but include predictable text that tells the story. These passages enable the examiner to gain additional insights into the more advanced emergent reading stages just outlined.

We recommend that examiners begin with these passages if the student's performance on the placement sentences (see the following instructions) suggests that the Level 1 passages may be too difficult. Explain to students at both the PP and P levels that the four pictures tell a story. Ask the student to look at all four pictures first, then retell the story by "reading" the pictures. We recommend that you transcribe the student's reading for later analysis. A tape recording of the session is quite helpful because you will probably have difficulty transcribing all that is said. If a student seems unable to tell a story from the pictures, ask the student to describe each picture. This will provide some insights into vocabulary knowledge, oral language skills, and whether a sense of story is developing. Further directions for administering Level PP and P passages and completing accompanying checklists are included with the assessment protocol forms (A and B) for each passage.

If the Student Cannot Read the Primer Level (P) Passages Adequately on the First Attempt . . . Then What?

Sometimes students making the developmental transition from advanced picture reading to early print reading are able to memorize text easily and repeat it verbatim, or nearly so. This sets up the opportunity for teaching them about one-to-one correspondence between spoken and written words and sounds. Therefore, if a student is unable to adequately read a passage aloud the first time, the examiner should read it aloud and then ask the student to try reading it again. If the student is able to do so, the examiner may assume that the student is transitioning into the early print reading stage. This would be a logical stopping point for the assessment.

INSTRUCTIONS FOR ADMINISTERING THE FORM E PASSAGES

In response to suggestions from educators, the inventory now includes a Form E. These passages are designed for students who read above the ninth-grade level. Each level (10, 11, 12) corresponds to that level of sophistication associated with high school reading. All three passages are expository in nature and are administered similarly to Form C passages. The one difference we recommend is that students not be required to read a portion of the passage orally. We believe that the oral reading skills of students in the 10th grade and above do not offer insightful assessment data. Rather, we believe that silent reading comprehension is the most important variable to be assessed at these levels. However, we have provided a miscue grid for each passage. Assessment of oral reading using this grid follows the guidelines discussed earlier.

SELECTED REFERENCES

Adams, M. J. (1994). *Beginning to read.* Cambridge, MA: MIT Press.

Betts, E. A. (1946). *Foundation of reading instruction.* New York: Academic Book Company.

Burke, C. (1987). Burke reading interview. In Y. Goodman, D. Watson, & C. Burke (Eds.), *Reading miscue inventory: Alternative procedures.* New York: Richard C. Owen.

Carroll, J. B. (1977). Developmental parameters of reading comprehension. In J. Guthrie (Ed.), *Cognition, curriculum, and comprehension.* Newark, DE: International Reading Association.

Clay, M. M. (1985). *The early detection of reading difficulties* (3rd ed.). Auckland, New Zealand: Heinemann.

Cochrane, O., Cochrane, D., Scalena, D., & Buchanan, E. (1984). *Reading, writing, and caring.* New York: Richard C. Owen.

Cooter, R. B., & Cooter, K. S. (1999). *Balanced literacy assessment milestones.* Dallas, TX: Unpublished manuscript.

Durrell, D. D. (1969). Listening comprehension versus reading comprehension. *Journal of Reading, 12,* 455–460.

Farr, R., & Tone, B. (1994). *Portfolio and performance assessment.* Fort Worth, TX: Harcourt Brace.

Fountas, I., & Pinnell, G. S. (1996). *Guided reading instruction: Good first teaching for all children.* Portsmouth, NH: Heinemann.

Fountas, I., & Pinnell, G. S. (1999). *Matching books to readers: Using leveled books in guided reading, K–3.* Portsmouth, NH: Heinemann.

Fountas, I., & Pinnell, G. S. (2000). *Guiding readers and writers (grades 3–6): Teaching comprehension, genre, and content literacy.* Portsmouth, NH: Heinemann.

Fountas, I., & Pinnell, G. S. (2001). *Leveled books for readers grades (3–6): A companion volume to guiding readers and writers.* Portsmouth, NH: Heinemann.

Fry, E. (1968). Readability formula that saves time. *Journal of Reading, 11,* 513–516, 575–578.

Harris, A. J., & Jacobson, M. D. (1975). The Harris-Jacobson readability formulas. In A. J. Harris & E. R. Sipay (Eds.), *How to increase reading ability* (pp. 712–729). New York: Longman.

Hill, B. C., & Ruptic, C. (1994). *Practical aspects of authentic assessment: Putting the pieces together.* Norwood, MA: Christopher-Gordon.

Holdaway, D. (1979). *Foundations of literacy.* Sydney, Australia: Ashton Scholastic.

Meyer, B. J. F., & Freedle, R. O. (1984). Effects of discourse type on recall. *American Educational Research Journal, 21*(1), 121–143.

Morrow, L. M. (1993). *Literacy development in the early years* (2nd ed.). Boston: Allyn & Bacon.

National Institute of Child Health and Human Development (NICHD). (2000). Report of the National Reading Panel: Teaching Children to Read. Washington, DC: NICHD. Available online at www.nationalreadingpanel.org

Piaget, J. (1955). *The language and thought of the child.* New York: World.

Powell, W. R. (1969). Reappraising the criteria for interpreting informal inventories. In D. DeBoer (Ed.), *Reading diagnosis and evaluation* (pp. 100–109). Newark, DE: International Reading Association.

Puckett, M. B., & Black, J. K. (1994). *Authentic assessment of the young child.* Upper Saddle River, NJ: Merrill/Prentice Hall.

Rasinski, T., & Padak, N. (2000). *Effective reading strategies: Teaching children who find reading difficult.* Upper Saddle River, NJ: Merrill/Prentice Hall.

Reutzel, D. R. (1999). On balanced reading. *The Reading Teacher, 52*(4), 2–4.

Reutzel, D. R., & Cooter, R. B. (2003). *Strategies for reading assessment and instruction: Helping every child succeed* (2nd ed.). Upper Saddle River, NJ: Merrill/Prentice Hall.

Reutzel, D. R., & Cooter, R. B. (2004). *Teaching children to read: Putting the pieces together* (4th ed.). Upper Saddle River, NJ: Merrill/Prentice Hall.

Rhodes, L. K., & Dudley-Marling, C. (1988). *Readers and writers with a difference.* Portsmouth, NH: Heinemann.

Rosenblatt, L. M. (1978). *The reader, the text, and the poem.* Carbondale, IL: Southern Illinois Press.

Sinatra, G. M. (1990). Convergence of listening and reading processing. *Reading Research Quarterly, 25*(2), 115–130.

Sulzby, E. (1985). Children's emergent reading of favorite storybooks. *Reading Research Quarterly, 20,* 458–481.

Valencia, S., & Pearson, P. D. (1987). Reading assessment: Time for a change. *The Reading Teacher, 40*(8), 726–733.

Vygotsky, L. S. (1962). *Mind in society.* Cambridge, MA: Harvard University Press.

SCORED STUDENT EXAMPLE

(pages 25–32)

The following pages provide an example of a completed student assessment. This particular example is based on the Level 5 passage found in Form A.

Audio Tape Example: An audiotape example is included in the 5th edition of the *Reading Inventory for the Classroom* for training purposes.

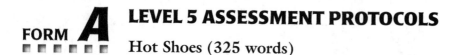
LEVEL 5 ASSESSMENT PROTOCOLS

Hot Shoes (325 words)

PART I: SILENT READING COMPREHENSION

Background Statement: "This story is about how one group of boys feel about their athletic shoes. Read this story to find out how important special shoes are to playing sports. Read it carefully because I will ask you to tell me about it when you finish."

Teacher Directions: Once the student completes the silent reading, say, "Tell me about the story you just read." Answers to the questions below that the student provides during the retelling should be marked "ua" in the appropriate blank to indicate that this response was unaided. Ask all remaining questions not addressed during the retelling and mark those the student answers with an "a" to indicate the correct response was given after prompting by the teacher.

Questions/Answers

Story Grammar Element/Level of Comprehension

_____ 1. Where did the story take place?
(*I. B. Belcher Elementary School or at a school*)

setting/literal
I don't remember

_a_ 2. Who were the two main characters in the story?
(*Jamie Lee and Josh Kidder*)

character-characterization/literal
Josh and Jane

_ua_ 3. What was the problem between Jamie and Josh?
(*Jamie didn't think Josh could be a good player
because of his shoes, Josh didn't fit in, or other
plausible responses*)

story problem(s)/inferential
*Jammie didn't like Josh because he had old shoes
and was different*

_____ 4. How did Josh solve his problem with the other boys?
(*he outplayed all of them*)

problem resolution/inferential
He ignored them

_____ 5. What kind of person was Jamie Lee?
(*conceited, stuck-up, or other plausible responses*)

character-characterization/evaluative
Tall ... a big tall boy

_a_ 6. What happened after the game?
(*the other boys gathered around and asked
Josh his secret*)

problem resolution attempts/literal
Everyone wanted to know how Josh learned to play so good

_ua_ 7. Why did everyone laugh when Josh said,
"Two things—lots of practice and cheap shoes"?
(*because everything had happened because of
his cheap shoes*)

problem resolution attempts/inferential
*It was funny. Because he played good even
with lousy shoes*

_____ 8. What lesson does this story teach?
(*responses will vary but should indicate a
theme/moral related to "it's not what you
wear that makes you good in a sport"*)

theme/evaluative
Josh was better than Jamie

PART II: ORAL READING AND ANALYSIS OF MISCUES

Directions: Say, "Now I would like to hear you read this story out loud." Have the student read orally until the 100-word sample is completed. Follow along on the Miscue Grid, marking any oral reading errors as appropriate. *Remember to count miscues only up to the point in the story containing the oral reading stop-marker (//).* Then complete the Developmental/Performance Summary (Part III) to determine whether to continue the assessment. (*Note:* The Miscue Grid should be completed after the assessment session has been concluded in order to minimize stress for the student.)

Hot Shoes

Text	mis-pronun.	sub-stitute	inser-tions	tchr. assist	omis-sions	Error Totals	Self-Correct.	(M) Meaning	(S) Syntax	(V) Visual
The guys at (the) I. B. Belcher										
Elementary School loved all the new sports [lived / so]		1			1		1	1	1	
shoes. Some were the "Sky High" [wib]	1									1
model by Leader. Others who really [buy]		1	1				1	1		
couldn't afford Sky Highs would settle		1					1	1		1
for a lesser shoe. Some liked the "Street [have]		1					1	1		1
Smarts" by master, or (the) [s]										
"Uptown-Downtown" by Beebop. [get]		1	1		1		1	1		1
The Belcher boys get to the point		1					1	1		1
with their shoes that they could										
identify their friends just by [impeas]	1								1	
looking at their feet. But the boy who [shoes / so]		1					1	1	1	
was the envy of the entire fifth [even]		1								
grade was Jamie Lee. He had a										
pair of "High Five Pump'em Ups"										
by Superior. The only thing Belcher										
boys // loved as much as their										
shoes was basketball.										
TOTALS	2	6	2	0	2		2	8	8	5

Summary of Reading Behaviors (Strengths and Needs)

PART III: MISCUE ANALYSIS

Directions: Circle all reading behaviors you observed.

A. Fundamental Behaviors Observed:

(L → R Directionality) (1 to 1 Matching) (Searching for Clues) Cross-Checking

B. Word Attack Behaviors:

No Attempt   Mispronunciation (Invented word)   (Substitutes)

Skips/Reads on   Asks for help   Repeats   (Attempts to Self-Correct)

("Sounds Out" (Segmenting))   Blends Sounds   Structural Analysis (Root words, Affixes)

C. Cueing Systems Used in Attempting Words

CUEING TOOL	MISCUE EXAMPLES	ACTUAL TEXT
(M) Meaning	8 of 12 miscues, M was used—(the, buy, have, -s, get, etc.)	
(S) Syntax	8 of 12 miscues, S was used—(same as M)	
(V) Visual	Only 5 of 12 miscues, V was used—Need to further check	

D. Fluency (word by word → fluent reading)

Word by Word _____   Mixed Phrasing ✓   Fluent Reading ✓   Fluency Rate in Seconds _140_

Performance Summary

Silent Reading Comprehension

_____ 0–1 questions missed = Easy

_____ 2 questions missed = Adequate

✓ 3+ questions missed = Too hard

Oral Reading Accuracy

_____ 0–1 oral error = Easy

_____ 2–5 oral errors = Adequate

✓ 6+ oral errors = Too hard

Continue to the next reading passage? _____ Yes ✓ No

PART IV: LISTENING COMPREHENSION

Directions: If you have decided not to continue to have the student read any other passages, then use this passage to begin assessing the student's listening comprehension (see page 19). Begin by reading the background statement for this passage and then say, "I am going to read this story to you. Please listen carefully because I will be asking you some questions after I finish reading it to you." After reading the passage, ask the student the questions associated with the passage. If the student correctly answers more than six questions, you will need to move to the next level and repeat the procedure.

Listening Comprehension

_6_ 0–2 questions missed = move to the next passage level

_7_ more than 2 questions missed = stop assessment or move down a level

Examiner's Notes:

Frank missed 3 comprehension questions at level 7, but only one at level 6. Therefore, his "reading capacity" is level 6.

STUDENT SUMMARY

[A blank Student Summary Form follows, additional blank forms appear in the Appendix; see p. 335.]

Student's Name   Frank Zevon

Examiner   K Spencer, 5th grade

Form(s) Used   (A)   B   C   D   E

I. Performance on Sentences for Passage Selection

__2__   Highest level with zero (0) errors

__4__   First level with two (2) or more errors

II. Overall Performance Levels on Reading Passages

	Narrative Passages (A, B)	Expository (Nonfiction) Passages (C, D, E)
Easy (Independent)	3	2
Adequate (Instructional)	4	3
Too hard (Frustration)	5	4
Average Reading Fluency Rate	130	100

III. Miscue Summary Chart

Directions: *Enter total number of miscues from ALL passages into each block indicated*

	Mispronunciation	Substitutions	Insertions	Teacher Assists	Omissions
Total Miscues from All Passages	4	11	3	2	2

(Purpose: To identify patterns of miscues based on highest frequency of errors to inform instructional decisions.)

IV. Error Analyses (Cueing Systems)

Directions: Enter total number of times (all passages) the student used each of the cueing systems when a miscue was made.

(Purpose: To determine the extent to which cueing systems are used to identify unknown words in print.)

Meaning Cues (M)   15

Syntax Cues (S)   14

Visual Cues (V)   1

V. Other Observations

The student had several repetitions, substitutions, and (logical) insertions. This may indicate he's using context rather well.

He does not regularly use visual cues when making miscues. This may indicate a need to review basic word attack strategies.

VI. Instructional Implications

1. Review the basic word attack strategy combining attention to: (1) context, (2) beginning sounds in words, and (3) ending sounds in words.

2. For comprehension development (narrative texts), review story grammers using "Literature Webs" strategy from Balanced Reading Strategies and Practices by Reutzel & Cooter (1999, Merrill Educ/Prentice Hall) on page 223.

STUDENT SUMMARY

Student's Name _____

Examiner _____

Form(s) Used   A   B   C   D   E

I. Performance on Sentences for Passage Selection

_____   Highest level with zero (0) errors

_____   First level with two (2) or more errors

II. Overall Performance Levels on Reading Passages

	Narrative Passages (A, B)	*Expository (Nonfiction) Passages (C, D, E)*
Easy (Independent)	_____	_____
Adequate (Instructional)	_____	_____
Too Hard (Frustration)	_____	_____
Average Reading Fluency Rate	_____	_____

III. Miscue Summary Chart

Directions: Enter total number of miscues from ALL passages into each block indicated.

	Mispronunciation	Substitutions	Insertions	Teacher Assists	Omissions
Total Miscues from All Passages					

(Purpose: To identify patterns of miscues based on highest frequency of errors to inform instructional decisions.)

IV. Error Analyses (Cueing Systems)

Directions: Enter total number of times (all passages) the student used each of the cueing systems when a miscue was made.

(Purpose: To determine the extent to which cueing systems are used to identify unknown words in print.)

Meaning Cues (M)   _____

Syntax Cues (S)   _____

Visual Cues (V)   _____

V. Other Observations

VI. Instructional Implications

A

SENTENCES FOR INITIAL PASSAGE SELECTION

FORM A: LEVEL 1

1. He wanted to fly.

2. The family got together.

3. The boy was jumping.

FORM A: LEVEL 2

1. I was walking fast to town.

2. She cried about going home.

3. I was pulled out of the hole.

FORM A: LEVEL 3

1. The forest was something to see.

2. I was enjoying sleeping when my Mom called.

3. I had to go to bed early last night.

FORM A: LEVEL 4

1. I dislike being the youngest.

2. I'm always getting into trouble.

3. They insisted on watching the show daily.

FORM A: LEVEL 5

1. Athletic shoes come in all kinds of colors.

2. Serious players manage to practice a lot.

3. A cheap pair of shoes doesn't last very long.

FORM A: LEVEL 6

1. He was searching for the evidence.

2. She realized the rock formations were too high.

3. The conservationist hoped to reforest the mountain.

FORM A: LEVEL 7

1. Unfortunately she was confused about the next activity.

2. The submerged rocks were dangerous.

3. She disappeared around the bend at a rapid rate.

FORM A: LEVEL 8

1. Ascending the mountain was rigorous and hazardous.

2. The cliff provided a panoramic view of the valley.

3. The incubation period lasted two weeks.

FORM A: LEVEL 9

1. The abduction made everyone suspicious.

2. The detective was besieged by the community.

3. Her pasty complexion made her look older.

NARRATIVE PASSAGES

The Accident

Let's Go Swimming

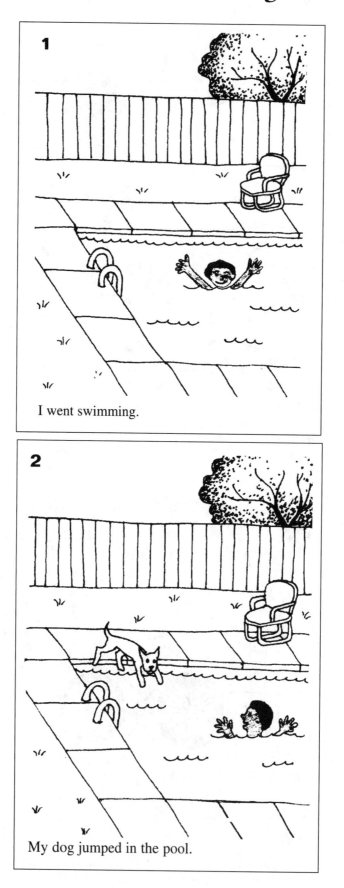

1

I went swimming.

2

My dog jumped in the pool.

3

My friends came over and jumped in
the pool too.

4

We had a great time swimming.

You Cannot Fly!

Once a boy named Sam wanted to fly.

His mother and father said, "You cannot fly."

His sister said, "You cannot fly."

Sam tried jumping off a box.

He tried jumping off his bed.

He fell down each time.

Sam still tried hard but he still could not fly.

Then one day a letter came for Sam.

The letter said, "Come and see me, Sam, on the next airplane."

It was from his grandfather.

Sam went to his family and read the letter.

Sam said, "Now I can fly."

Sam and his family all laughed together.

The Pig and the Snake

One day Mr. Pig was walking to town.

He saw a big hole in the road.

A big snake was in the hole.

"Help me," said the snake, "and I will be your friend."

"No, no," said Mr. Pig. "If I help you get out, you will bite me. You are a snake!"

The snake cried and cried.

So Mr. Pig pulled the snake out of the hole.

Then the snake said, "Now I am going to bite you, Mr. Pig."

"How can you bite me after I helped you out of the hole?" said Mr. Pig.

The snake said, "You knew I was a snake when you pulled me out!"

The Big Bad Wolf

One day Mr. Wolf was walking through the forest. He was enjoying an afternoon walk and not bothering anyone. All of a sudden it started to rain and he became wet and cold.

Just when Mr. Wolf was about to freeze to death, he saw a small house in the woods. Smoke was coming from the chimney, so he knocked on the door. No one was home, but a note on the door said

Come in and make yourself warm. I'll be back about 2:00 p.m.

Love,

Granny

The poor wet wolf came in and began to warm himself by the fire He saw one of Granny's nightgowns on the bed, so he decided to p it on instead of his wet clothes. Since he was still very, very cold, he decided to get into Granny's bed. Soon he was fast asleep.

Mr. Wolf fell into a deep sleep. When he awoke, Mr. Wolf found an old woman, a little girl wearing a red coat, and a woodcutter standing around the bed. The woodcutter was yelling at Mr. Wolf and saying something about how he was going to kill him with his axe. Mr. Wolf jumped out of the bed and ran for his life.

Later that day, Mr. Wolf was finally safe at home. His wife said, "Just you wait, those humans will make up a story about how big and bad *you* were."

New Clothes

Bobby was the youngest member of his family. He didn't like being the youngest because he couldn't stay up late and watch television. Most of all, he disliked having to wear hand-me-down clothes from his brother.

One day Bobby went to his mother and said, "Mom, I'm tired o wearing Brad's clothes. Why can't I have some more new clothes th school year?"

His mother replied, "Bobby, you know we can't afford to buy even more new clothes. You should be happy with the new clothes we have already bought. Besides, most of Brad's clothes are just like new."

As Bobby walked away, his mother said, "Bobby, if you can find way to earn some money, I'll see what I can do to help you get wha you want."

Bobby thought and thought. Finally, an idea hit him. Brad and h sister, Sara, had part-time jobs, and they didn't always have time to do their work around the house. What if he did some of their work for a small fee?

Bobby approached Brad and Sara about his idea. They liked his idea and agreed to pay Bobby for cleaning their rooms and making their beds.

As Bobby turned to leave the room, Sara said, "Bobby, do a good job or we will have to cut back how much we pay you."

Bobby took care of his brother's and sister's rooms for four weeks. Finally on the last Saturday before school started, Bobby's mom took him to the mall. Bobby got to pick out a cool pair of baggy jeans and a new shirt. On the first day of school, Bobby felt proud of his new clothes that he had worked so hard to buy. His mother was even prouder.

Hot Shoes

The guys at the I. B. Belcher Elementary School loved all the new sport shoes. Some wore the "Sky High" model by Leader. Others who couldn't afford Sky Highs would settle for a lesser shoe. Some liked the "Street Smarts" by Master, or the "Uptown-Downtown" by Beebop. The Belcher boys got to the point with their shoes that they could identify their friends just by looking at their feet. But the boy who was the envy of the entire fifth grade was Jamie Lee. He had a pair of "High Five Pump'em Ups" by Superior. The only thing Belcher boys loved as much as their shoes was basketball. They would lace up their fancy athletic shoes and play basketball all afternoon. Everyone was sure that the shoes helped them jump higher and run faster.

One day a new student showed up on the playground. His name was Josh Kidder, and no one knew him. He lived in the poor part of town and wore a cheap pair of black hightop tennis shoes. They were made by an old fashioned company called White Dot. When Jamie Lee saw Josh's White Dot shoes, he said, "No serious basketball player wears White Dots. Where have you been, Kidder?" Josh said, "Well, I may not have a pair of shoes like yours but I would like to play basketball with you and the other guys."

Jamie Lee and the other boys kind of chuckled and said, "Sure kid, no problem." What happened next is a matter of history now at I. B. Belcher School. Josh ran faster, jumped higher, and scored more points (35 points to be exact) than anybody else that day. Jamie Lee, whom Josh guarded, only managed two points.

When it was all over the boys gathered around Josh. He was the hero of the day. "What's your secret weapon?" asked Randy. Josh just smiled and said, "Two things—lots of practice and cheap shoes." Everyone laughed.

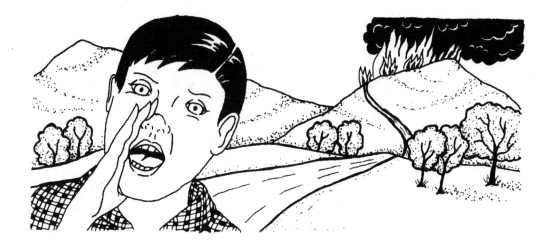

Mountain Fire

One August afternoon Brad and Kevin went tracking with their fathers on Mount Holyoak. Brad's father was a conservationist for the Forest Service and was searching for evidence of cougars. Many people feared that the cougars were extinct on Mount Holyoak. The boys became excited when they found what appeared to be a partial cougar track near a stream. But as the day wore on, no new tracks were found.

After lunch Brad's father sent the boys upstream while he circled west. He told the boys to return to the lunch site in an hour. After about forty-five minutes, the boys found the stream's source and could follow it no more. They decided to search close to the stream before starting back. They saw interesting rock formations, eagles' nests on high ledges and, finally, two fresh cougar footprints. Both boys were very excited until they realized that they no longer could hear the stream. They were lost.

The boys searched an hour or more for the mountain stream, but without success. They were tired, dirty, and getting worried. Brad decided to start a small fire in hopes of his father seeing the smoke. Kevin reminded Brad of the danger of forest fires but finally agreed to help collect the twigs, branches, and brush. The moment Brad struck a match in the extra-dry mountain air and stuck it to the dry tinder, the fire exploded into a large fireball.

In a matter of minutes, trees all around the boys burst into flames. The fire spread quickly up the mountainside. The boys ran downhill as fast as they could.

Before the day was out, hotshot crews, airplanes carrying fire retardants, and bucket-loaded helicopters were on the scene trying to contain the fire. The fire raged for days, however, and by the time it was put out, more than 45,000 acres of timber had been consumed.

For several years Brad and Kevin spent every spare moment helping to reforest the mountain. One day the forest ranger commented, "Well, boys, it looks like things are about back to normal." Brad looked down at his feet and sadly replied, "Maybe, but no new cougar tracks have been seen since the fire."

The Canoe Trip

Katherine and her family like to spend their vacation camping out. Frequently they go to either Great Smoky Mountains National Park or Yellowstone National Park. Since they have camped out for many years, they have become quite accomplished. Katherine is able to start a fire with flint and steel, build a lean-to for shelter, and find food in the forest on which to live.

Katherine's favorite outdoor activity is canoeing. Although she is quite a good canoer, there is one canoe trip that she'll never forget. It was a canoe trip she took with her family and her friend Amy down the Madison River near West Yellowstone.

Katherine and Amy were in a canoe together following her parents down the river. The early going was fine, and they didn't have any major problems. The girls did get confused once or twice in their steering, and the boat would go sideways. But after about thirty minutes on the river, Katherine and Amy felt secure about their ability to navigate. Unfortunately their canoe could not keep up with Katherine's parents' canoe because they were carrying all the rations in two coolers. Slowly the lead canoe disappeared around a bend.

When the girls' canoe rounded a bend, not only could they not see the lead canoe but they were heading directly into some rough white water. The rough water was swift and there were a lot of rocks submerged below the surface. The swiftness and rocks were causing problems for the jittery canoe and the two inexperienced girls.

Just as the canoe was about to clear the rough water, it struck a large boulder just beneath the surface. Before the girls knew what had happened, the canoe had capsized, sending them into the icy cold river. Naturally they had on life jackets so they were not in much danger. But the two coolers full of food and the canoe started floating away from them at a rapid rate.

Katherine managed to grab hold of the canoe and one paddle. Amy swam over to the shore. After much effort both girls managed to pull in the canoe, empty the water, and start downstream after the lost coolers. But since they had only one paddle they limped along, unable to catch up to the now disappeared coolers.

Some forty-five minutes later, feeling cold and upset, the girls rounded a sharp bend in the river. To their surprise they saw the rest of the family sitting on the south-side shore of the river. Katherine's Dad had built a fire and was roasting hot dogs. Katherine's mother and little brother were sitting on the two coolers eating a hot dog and munching on potato chips. Dad said, "What took you two so long? We didn't know you were going to stop and take a swim, but thanks for sending the food on ahead." As cold as they were, Katherine and Amy couldn't help but laugh.

The Eagle

There exists an old Native American legend about an eagle who thought he was a chicken. It seems that a Hopi farmer and his only son decided to climb a nearby mountain to observe an eagle's nest. The trip would take them all day, so they brought along some rations and water for the trek. The man and the boy crossed the enormous fields of maize and beans into the foothills. Soon thereafter they were ascending the mountain, and the climb became rigorous and hazardous They occasionally looked back toward their home and at the panoramic view of the entire valley.

Finally the farmer and son reached the mountain's summit. Perched on the highest point on a ledge was the eagle's nest. The farmer reached his hand into the nest after realizing that the mother had gone in search of food. He brought out a most precious prize, an eagle's egg. He tucked it into his tunic and the two descended the mount.

The egg was placed in the nest of a chicken for incubation. It soon hatched. The eaglet grew with the baby chicks and adopted their habits for gathering food in the barnyard—namely, scratching for feed the farmer threw out.

Some time later an Anasazi brave passed through the area and saw this enormous brown eagle scratching and walking about in the barnyard. He dismounted from his horse and went to the farmer. "Why do you have an eagle acting as a chicken? It is not right," queried the noble brave.

"That's no eagle, it's a chicken," retorted the farmer. "Can't you see that it scratches for food with the other chickens? No, it is indeed a chicken," exclaimed the farmer.

"I will show you that this is an eagle," said the brave.

The brave took the eagle on his arm and climbed to the top of the barn. Then saying, "You are an eagle, the most noble of birds. Fly and soar as you were destined!" He threw the eagle from the barn. But the startled eagle fluttered to the ground and began pecking for food.

"See," said the farmer. "told you it is a chicken."

The brave replied, "I'll show you this is an eagle. It is clear what I must do."

Again the brave took the eagle on his arm and began walking toward the mountain. He climbed all day until he reached a high bluff overlooking the valley. Then the brave, with outstretched arm, held the bird out and said, "You are an eagle, the most noble of birds. Fly and soar as you were destined to."

Just then a mountain breeze washed across the eagle. His eyes brightened as he caught the wild scent of freedom. In a moment the eagle stretched his mighty wings and let out a magnificent screech. Leaping from the brave's arm, he flew high into the western sky.

The eagle saw more of the world in that one great moment than his barnyard friends would discover in a lifetime.

The Case of Angela Violet

Angela Violet was an elderly lady in our neighborhood who some people thought suspicious. She was rarely seen outside her spacious Victorian-styled home, and then only to retrieve the daily mail. Her pasty complexion and ancient dress made her appear like an apparition. Small children in the neighborhood speculated that she might be some sort of witch. It appeared that Miss Violet had no contact with the outside world.

One autumn day news spread through the community that a high school cheerleader, Katrina Bowers, had disappeared. The police feared that Katrina had been abducted. State and local police joined forces with the Federal Bureau of Investigation in the massive search effort. In spite of all the best efforts in the constabulary, no trace of Katrina Bowers was uncovered. After ten days of suspense and worry, the search was called off.

Three weeks after Katrina's apparent abduction a break in the case occurred. An anonymous telephone caller informed the police that Miss Angela Violet had kidnapped Katrina. It was alleged that Miss Violet was holding her captive in her basement. Because of Miss Violet's unusual lifestyle, the police were inclined to give some credence to the tip. A search warrant was issued and the police converged on her house.

Detective Donna Jordan knocked on the shabby door of Miss Violet's residence. Two other officers attended Detective Jordan. Miss Violet showed surprise but welcomed the police into her home graciously. She consented to having her home searched.

By the time the police had completed their search, two television news trucks had taken position outside her home. When the detectives came out of the house without Miss Violet, the anxious newspeople besieged them with queries.

Detective Jordan stepped forward and calmly said, "What we found was a kindly lady who is caring night and day for her ailing mother. There is no evidence whatsoever that Miss Violet has any involvement in the Katrina Bowers case."

People in the community began to reach out to Miss Violet and her mother from then on. They took food and sat with Miss Violet's mother so she could get out more. As for Katrina Bowers, she was located safe and sound in California with relatives. She had been a runaway case.

EXAMINER'S
ASSESSMENT PROTOCOLS

PREPRIMER (PP) LEVEL ASSESSMENT PROTOCOLS

The Accident (Wordless picture story)

PART I: WORDLESS PICTURE STORY READING

Background Statement: "These pictures tell a story about a girl and something that happened to her. Look at each picture as I show it to you and think about the story the pictures tell. Later, I will want you to tell me the story using the pictures."

Teacher Directions: Refer the student to each picture slowly and in order as numbered. Do not comment on the pictures. Then repeat the procedure, asking the student to tell the story in the student's own words. Record the student's reading using a tape recorder, and transcribe the reading as it is being dictated. Replay the recording later to make sure that your transcription is accurate and complete.

PART II: EMERGENT READING BEHAVIOR CHECKLIST

Directions: Following are emergent reading behaviors identified through research and grouped according to broad developmental stages. Check all behaviors you have observed. *If the student progresses to Stage 3 or 4, continue your assessment using the Primer Level (P) passage.*

Stage 1: Early Connections to Reading—Describing Pictures

_____ Attends to and describes (labels) pictures in books

_____ Has a limited sense of story

_____ Follows verbal directions for this activity

_____ Uses oral vocabulary appropriate for age/grade level

_____ Displays attention span appropriate for age/grade level

_____ Responds to questions in an appropriate manner

_____ Appears to connect pictures (sees as being interrelated)

Stage 2: Connecting Pictures to Form a Story

_____ Attends to pictures and develops oral stories.

_____ Uses only childlike or descriptive (storyteller) language to tell the story, rather than book language (i.e., Once upon a time . . . ; There once was a little boy . . .)

Stage 3: Transitional Picture Reading

_____ Attends to pictures as a connected story

_____ Mixes storyteller language with book language

Stage 4: Advanced Picture Reading

_____ Attends to pictures and develops oral stories

_____ Speaks as though reading the story (uses book language)

Examiner's Notes:

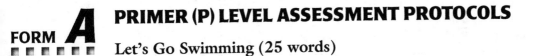

PART I: PICTURE STORY READING–ORAL READING AND ANALYSIS OF MISCUES

Background Statement: "This is a story about a child having fun. Let's look at each picture first. Now, read the story to yourself. Later, I will want you to read the story to me."

Teacher Directions: Refer the student to each frame of the story slowly and in order as numbered. Do not read the story or comment on the pictures. After the student has read the story silently, ask the student to read the story aloud. Record the student's reading using a tape recorder, and mark any miscues on the Miscue Grid provided. Following the oral reading, complete the Emergent Reading Behavior Checklist. Assessment information obtained from both the Miscue Grid and the Emergent Reading Behavior Checklist will help you determine whether to continue your assessment. If the student is unable to read the passage independently the first time, read it aloud, then ask the student to try to read the story again. This will help you understand whether the student is able to memorize and repeat text, an important developmental milestone (see the Instructions for Administering the Preprimer (PP) and Primer (P) Passages section on page 20 for more information). The assessment should stop after this activity, if the child is unable to read the text independently. (*Note:* The Miscue Grid should be completed *after* the assessment session has been concluded in order to minimize stress for the student.)

ERROR TYPES   **ERROR ANALYSIS**

	mis-pronun.	sub-stitute	inser-tions	tchr. assist	omis-sions	Error Totals	Self-Correct.	(M) Meaning	(S) Syntax	(V) Visual
Let's Go Swimming										
I went swimming.										
My dog jumped in the pool.										
My friends came over and										
jumped in the pool too.										
We had a great time swimming.										
TOTALS										

Summary of Reading Behaviors (Strengths and Needs)

PART II: EMERGENT READING BEHAVIOR CHECKLIST

Directions: Following are emergent reading behaviors identified through research and grouped according to broad developmental stages. After the student has completed the oral reading, check each behavior observed below to help determine development level and whether to continue the assessment. *If the student seems to be at Stage 6 or 7 and the oral reading scored at an Easy or Adequate level, continue the assessment using the Level 1 passage.*

Stage 5: Early Print Reading

_____ Tells a story using the pictures

_____ Knows print moves from left to right, top to bottom

_____ Creates part of the text using book language and knows some words on sight

Stage 6: Early Strategic Reading

_____ Uses context to guess at some unknown words (guesses make sense)

_____ Notices beginning sounds in words and uses them in guessing unknown words

_____ Seems to sometimes use syntax to help identify words in print

_____ Recognizes some word parts, such as root words and affixes

Stage 7: Moderate Strategic Reading

_____ Sometimes uses context and word parts to decode words

_____ Self-corrects when making an oral reading miscue

_____ Retells the passage easily and may embellish the story line

_____ Shows some awareness of vowel sounds

Examiner's Notes:

PART III: DEVELOPMENTAL/PERFORMANCE SUMMARY

Oral Reading Accuracy

_____ 0–1 oral errors = Easy

_____ 2–5 oral errors = Adequate

_____ 6+ oral errors = Too hard

Continue to the next assessment level passage? _____ Yes _____ No

Examiner's Notes:

LEVEL 1 ASSESSMENT PROTOCOLS

You Cannot Fly! (96 words)

PART I: SILENT READING COMPREHENSION

Background Statement: "Have you ever wished you could fly? A boy named Sam in this story wants to fly. Read this story to find out if Sam gets to fly. Read it carefully because when you're through I'm going to ask you to tell me about the story."

Teacher Directions: Once the student completes the silent reading, say, "Tell me about the story you just read." Answers to the questions below that the student provides during the retelling should be marked "ua" in the appropriate blank to indicate that this response was unaided. Ask all remaining questions not addressed during the retelling and mark those the student answers with an "a" to indicate that the correct response was given after prompting by the teacher.

Questions/Answers	*Story Grammar Element/ Level of Comprehension*
_____ 1. What was the name of the boy in the story? *(Sam)*	character-characterization/literal
_____ 2. What did Sam really want to do? *(Sam wanted to fly, but couldn't)*	story problem(s)/literal
_____ 3. What were two ways Sam tried to fly? *(jumping off his bed and a box)*	problem resolution attempts/literal
_____ 4. How was Sam's problem finally solved? *(Sam got to ride on an airplane)*	problem resolution/inferential
_____ 5. What did the family and Sam do after reading the letter? *(laughed)*	problem resolution attempts/literal
_____ 6. Where did the story take place? *(Sam's house)*	setting/inferential
_____ 7. What did Sam learn about being able to fly? *(people can't fly except in airplanes)*	theme/evaluative
_____ 8. What words would you use to tell someone what kind of boy Sam was? *(responses will vary; accept plausible ones)*	character-characterization/evaluative

PART II: ORAL READING AND ANALYSIS OF MISCUES

Directions: Say, "Now I would like to hear you read this story out loud. Please start at the beginning and keep reading until I tell you to stop." *Have the student read orally until the oral reading stop-marker (//) is reached.* Follow along on the Miscue Grid, marking any oral reading errors as appropriate. Then complete the Performance Summary to determine whether to continue the assessment. (*Note:* The Miscue Grid should be completed *after* the assessment session has been concluded in order to minimize stress for the student.)

ERROR TYPES

ERROR ANALYSIS

You Cannot Fly!

	mis-pronun.	sub-stitute	inser-tions	tchr. assist	omis-sions	Error Totals	Self-Correct.	(M) Meaning	(S) Syntax	(V) Visual
Once a boy named Sam wanted to										
fly. His mother and father said,										
"You cannot fly." His sister said,										
"You cannot fly." Sam tried jumping										
off a box. He tried jumping off										
his bed. He fell down each time.										
Sam still tried hard but he still										
could not fly. Then one day										
a letter came for Sam. The letter										
said, "Come and see me, Sam, on										
the next airplane." It was from										
his grandfather. Sam went to his										
family and read the letter. Sam										
said, "Now I can fly." Sam and his										
family all laughed together.//										
TOTALS										

Summary of Reading Behaviors (Strengths and Needs)

PART III: MISCUE ANALYSIS

Directions: *Circle all reading behaviors you observed.*

A. Fundamental Behaviors Observed:

L → R Directionality   1 to 1 Matching   Searching for Clues   Cross-Checking

B. Word Attack Behaviors:

No Attempt   Mispronunciation (Invented word)   Substitutes

Skips/Reads On   Asks for Help   Repeats   Attempts to Self-Correct

"Sounds Out" (Segmenting)   Blends Sounds   Structural Analysis (Root words, Affixes)

C. Cueing Systems Used in Attempting Words

CUEING TOOL	MISCUE EXAMPLES	ACTUAL TEXT
(M) Meaning		
(S) Syntax		
(V) Visual		

D. Fluency (word by word → fluent reading)

Word by Word _____   Mixed Phrasing _____   Fluent Reading _____   Fluency Rate in Seconds _____

Performance Summary

Silent Reading Comprehension

_____ 0–1 questions missed = Easy

_____ 2 questions missed = Adequate

_____ 3+ questions missed = Too hard

Oral Reading Accuracy

_____ 0–1 oral error = Easy

_____ 2–5 oral errors = Adequate

_____ 6+ oral errors = Too hard

Continue to the next reading passage? _____ Yes   _____ No

PART IV: LISTENING COMPREHENSION

Directions: If you have decided not to continue to have the student read any other passages, then use this passage to begin assessing the student's listening comprehension (see page 19). Begin by reading the background statement for this passage and then say, "I am going to read this story to you. Please listen carefully because I will be asking you some questions after I finish reading it to you." After reading the passage, ask the student the questions associated with the passage. If the student correctly answers more than six questions, you will need to move to the next level and repeat the procedure.

Listening Comprehension

_____ 0–2 questions missed = move to the next passage level

_____ more than 2 questions missed = stop assessment or move down a level

Examiner's Notes:

LEVEL 2 ASSESSMENT PROTOCOLS

The Pig and the Snake (111 words)

PART I: SILENT READING COMPREHENSION

Background Statement: "Read this story to find out what happened to Mr. Pig when he tried to help a snake in trouble. Be sure and read it carefully because I'm going to ask you to tell me about the story."

Teacher Directions: Once the student completes the silent reading, say, "Tell me about the story you just read." Answers to the questions below that the student provides during the retelling should be marked "ua" in the appropriate blank to indicate that this response was unaided. Ask all remaining questions not addressed during the retelling and mark those the student answers with an "a" to indicate that the correct response was given after prompting by the teacher.

Questions/Answers	Story Grammar Element/ Level of Comprehension
_____ 1. Where did the story take place? *(on the road to town)*	setting/literal
_____ 2. Who were the animals in the story? *(Mr. Pig and a snake)*	character-characterization/literal
_____ 3. What was the snake's problem? *(he was stuck in a hole and wanted help getting out)*	story problem(s)/literal
_____ 4. How did the snake solve his problem? *(by getting the pig to help him by promising not to hurt him)*	problem resolution/inferential
_____ 5. What words would you use to describe the snake? *(sneaky, liar, or any other plausible response)*	character-characterization/evaluative
_____ 6. What lesson did Mr. Pig learn? *(responses will vary but should indicate a theme/moral related to "you can't always trust what someone says")*	theme/evaluative
_____ 7. How did Mr. Pig feel after he helped pull the snake out of the hole? *(surprised, upset, etc.)*	character-characterization/inferential
_____ 8. What was one thing the snake did to get Mr. Pig to help him out of the hole? *(cried or said he would be his friend)*	problem resolution attempts/literal

PART II: ORAL READING AND ANALYSIS OF MISCUES

Directions: Say, "Now I would like to hear you read this story out loud." Have the student read orally until the 100-word sample is completed. Follow along on the Miscue Grid, marking any oral reading errors as appropriate. *Remember to count miscues only up to the point in the story containing the oral reading stop-marker (///).* Then complete the Developmental/Performance Summary to determine whether to continue the assessment. (*Note:* The Miscue Grid should be completed *after* the assessment session has been concluded in order to minimize stress for the student.)

ERROR TYPES

ERROR ANALYSIS

The Pig and the Snake	mis-pronun.	sub-stitute	inser-tions	tchr. assist	omis-sions	Error Totals	Self-Correct.	(M) Meaning	(S) Syntax	(V) Visual
One day Mr. Pig was walking to										
town. He saw a big hole in the										
road. A big snake was in the										
hole. "Help me," said the snake,										
"and I will be your friend." "No, no,"										
said Mr. Pig. "If I help you get										
out, you will bite me. You are										
a snake!" The snake cried and										
cried. So Mr. Pig pulled the										
snake out of the hole.										
Then the snake said, "Now I am										
going to bite you, Mr. Pig."										
"How can you bite me after										
I helped you out of the hole?"										
said Mr. Pig. The snake said,//										
"You knew I was a snake										
when you pulled me out!"										
TOTALS										

Summary of Reading Behaviors (Strengths and Needs)

PART III: MISCUE ANALYSIS

Directions: *Circle all reading behaviors you observed.*

A. Fundamental Behaviors Observed:

L → R Directionality   1 to 1 Matching   Searching for Clues   Cross-Checking

B. Word Attack Behaviors:

No Attempt   Mispronunciation (Invented word)   Substitutes

Skips/Reads On   Asks for Help   Repeats   Attempts to Self-Correct

"Sounds Out" (Segmenting)   Blends Sounds   Structural Analysis (Root words, Affixes)

C. Cueing Systems Used in Attempting Words

CUEING TOOL	MISCUE EXAMPLES	ACTUAL TEXT
(M) Meaning		
(S) Syntax		
(V) Visual		

D. Fluency (word by word → fluent reading)

Word by Word _____   Mixed Phrasing _____   Fluent Reading _____   Fluency Rate in Seconds _____

Performance Summary

Silent Reading Comprehension

_____ 0–1 questions missed = Easy

_____ 2 questions missed = Adequate

_____ 3+ questions missed = Too hard

Oral Reading Accuracy

_____ 0–1 oral error = Easy

_____ 2–5 oral errors = Adequate

_____ 6+ oral errors = Too hard

Continue to the next reading passage? _____ Yes _____ No

PART IV: LISTENING COMPREHENSION

Directions: If you have decided not to continue to have the student read any other passages, then use this passage to begin assessing the student's listening comprehension (see page 19). Begin by reading the background statement for this passage and then say, "I am going to read this story to you. Please listen carefully because I will be asking you some questions after I finish reading it to you." After reading the passage, ask the student the questions associated with the passage. If the student correctly answers more than six questions, you will need to move to the next level and repeat the procedure.

Listening Comprehension

_____ 0–2 questions missed = move to the next passage level

_____ more than 2 questions missed = stop assessment or move down a level

Examiner's Notes:

LEVEL 3 ASSESSMENT PROTOCOLS

The Big Bad Wolf (235 words)

PART I: SILENT READING COMPREHENSION

Background Statement: "Have you ever had someone say something about you that wasn't true? Mr. Wolf thinks he has. Read and find out what really happened. Read it carefully because I'm going to ask you to tell me about the story."

Teacher Directions: Once the student completes the silent reading, say "Tell me about the story you just read." Answers to the questions below that the student provides during the retelling should be marked "ua" in the appropriate blank to indicate that this response was unaided. Ask all remaining questions not addressed during the retelling and mark those the student answers with an "a" to indicate that the correct response was given after prompting by the teacher.

	Questions/Answers	*Story Grammar Element/ Level of Comprehension*
_____	1. Who was the story about? (*Mr. Wolf, Granny, little girl, woodcutter*)	character-characterization/literal
_____	2. Where was Mr. Wolf when he saw the house? (*in the forest*)	setting/literal
_____	3. Why did Mr. Wolf need to get into the house? (*he was wet and freezing*)	story problem(s)/literal
_____	4. What made Mr. Wolf think it was OK to go into the house? (*the note on the door*)	problem resolution attempts/inferential
_____	5. What did Mr. Wolf do after entering the house? (*began to warm himself and changed into a nightgown*)	problem resolution attempts/literal
_____	6. Why did Mr. Wolf have to run for his life? (*woodcutter was going to kill him*)	problem resolution attempts/literal
_____	7. What lesson did Mr. Wolf learn? (*responses will vary but should indicate a theme/moral related to not doing things without permission*)	theme/evaluative
_____	8. What did Mrs. Wolf say that would make you think she didn't trust humans? (*she said the humans would make up a story about her husband*)	character-characterization/inferential

PART II: ORAL READING AND ANALYSIS OF MISCUES

Directions: Say, "Now I would like to hear you read this story out loud." Have the student read orally until the 100-word sample is completed. Follow along on the Miscue Grid, marking any oral reading errors as appropriate. *Remember to count miscues only up to the point in the story containing the oral reading stop-marker (//).* Then complete the Developmental/Performance Summary to determine whether to continue the assessment. (*Note:* The Miscue Grid should be completed *after* the assessment session has been concluded in order to minimize stress for the student.)

ERROR TYPES | ERROR ANALYSIS

The Big Bad Wolf	mis-pronun.	sub-stitute	inser-tions	tchr. assist	omis-sions	Error Totals	Self-Correct.	(M) Meaning	(S) Syntax	(V) Visual
One day Mr. Wolf was walking										
through the forest. He was enjoying										
an afternoon walk and not bothering										
anyone. All of a sudden it starred										
to rain and he became wet and cold.										
Just when Mr. Wolf was about										
to freeze to death, he saw a small										
house in the woods. Smoke was										
coming from the chimney, so he										
knocked on the door. No one was										
home, but a note on the door said:										
Come in and make yourself warm. I'll be back about 2:00 p.m.										
Love,										
Granny										
The poor wet wolf came in and										
began to warm himself by // *the*										
fire.										
TOTALS										

Summary of Reading Behaviors (Strengths and Needs)

PART III: MISCUE ANALYSIS

Directions: *Circle all reading behaviors you observed.*

A. Fundamental Behaviors Observed:

L → R Directionality   1 to 1 Matching   Searching for Clues   Cross-Checking

B. Word Attack Behaviors:

No Attempt   Mispronunciation (Invented word)   Substitutes

Skips/Reads On   Asks for Help   Repeats   Attempts to Self-Correct

"Sounds Out" (Segmenting)   Blends Sounds   Structural Analysis (Root words, Affixes)

C. Cueing Systems Used in Attempting Words

CUEING TOOL	MISCUE EXAMPLES	ACTUAL TEXT
(M) Meaning		
(S) Syntax		
(V) Visual		

D. Fluency (word by word → fluent reading)

Word by Word _____   Mixed Phrasing _____   Fluent Reading _____   Fluency Rate in Seconds _____

Performance Summary

Silent Reading Comprehension

_____ 0–1 questions missed = Easy

_____ 2 questions missed = Adequate

_____ 3+ questions missed = Too hard

Oral Reading Accuracy

_____ 0–1 oral error = Easy

_____ 2–5 oral errors = Adequate

_____ 6+ oral errors = Too hard

Continue to the next reading passage? _____ Yes   _____ No

PART IV: LISTENING COMPREHENSION

Directions: If you have decided not to continue to have the student read any other passages, then use this passage to begin assessing the student's listening comprehension (see page 19). Begin by reading the background statement for this passage and then say, "I am going to read this story to you. Please listen carefully because I will be asking you some questions after I finish reading it to you." After reading the passage, ask the student the questions associated with the passage. If the student correctly answers more than six questions, you will need to move to the next level and repeat the procedure.

Listening Comprehension

_____ 0–2 questions missed = move to the next passage level

_____ more than 2 questions missed = stop assessment or move down a level

Examiner's Notes:

LEVEL 4 ASSESSMENT PROTOCOLS

New Clothes (295 words)

PART I: SILENT READING COMPREHENSION

Background Statement: "Read this story to find out what happens when Bobby decides he wants some new clothes. Be sure and read it carefully because I'm going to ask you to tell me about the story when you finish."

Teacher Directions: Once the student completes the silent reading, say, "Tell me about the story you just read." Answers to the questions below that the student provides during the retelling should be marked "ua" in the appropriate blank to indicate that this response was unaided. Ask all remaining questions not addressed during the retelling and mark those the student answers with an "a" to indicate that the correct response was given after prompting by the teacher.

Questions/Answers	*Story Grammar Element/ Level of Comprehension*
_____ 1. Who are the characters in this story? *(Bobby, Mother, Sara, and Brad)*	character-characterization/literal
_____ 2. Where does the story mainly take place? *(Bobby's home)*	setting/literal
_____ 3. Besides being the youngest, what is Bobby's big problem in the story? *(earning money to buy new clothes)*	story problem(s)/literal
_____ 4. What did Bobby do to earn money? *(he cleaned his brother's and sister's rooms)*	problem resolution/literal
_____ 5. Besides hand-me-down clothes, what was one other thing that Bobby disliked about being the youngest? *(couldn't stay up late and watch TV)*	story problem(s)/literal
_____ 6. What does Bobby do at the end of the story? *(buys some new clothes)*	problem resolution/literal
_____ 7. What would be some words, other than proud, that would describe how Bobby felt on the first day of school? *(happy, cool, other plausible responses)*	character-characterization/ evaluative
_____ 8. Why do you think Bobby's mother was "even prouder"? *(responses should indicate that Bobby's mother was proud that her son had worked hard and found a way to earn money)*	character-characterization

PART II: ORAL READING AND ANALYSIS OF MISCUES

Directions: Say, "Now I would like to hear you read some of this story out loud." Have the student read orally until the 100-word sample is completed. Follow along on the Miscue Grid, marking any oral reading errors as appropriate. *Remember to count miscues only up to the point in the story containing the oral reading stop-marker (//).* Then complete the Developmental/Performance Summary to determine whether to continue the assessment. (*Note:* The Miscue Grid should be completed *after* the assessment session has been concluded in order to minimize stress for the student.)

ERROR TYPES

	mis-pronun.	sub-stitute	inser-tions	tchr. assist	omis-sions	Error Totals	Self-Correct.	(M) Meaning	(S) Syntax	(V) Visual
New Clothes										
Bobby was the youngest member										
of his family. He didn't like being										
the youngest because he couldn't										
stay up late and watch television.										
Most of all, he disliked having to										
wear hand-me-down clothes from										
his brother. One day Bobby went										
to his mother and said, "Mom,										
I'm tired of wearing Brad's										
clothes. Why can't I have										
some more new clothes this										
school year?" His mother replied,										
"Bobby, you know we can't										
afford to buy even more new clothes.										
You should be happy with the new										
clothes we have already bought.										
Besides, most of Brad's clothes										
are just like // *new*."										
TOTALS										

Summary of Reading Behaviors (Strengths and Needs)

PART III: MISCUE ANALYSIS

Directions: Circle all reading behaviors you observed.

A. Fundamental Behaviors Observed:

L → R Directionality   1 to 1 Matching   Searching for Clues   Cross-Checking

B. Word Attack Behaviors:

No Attempt   Mispronunciation (Invented word)   Substitutes

Skips/Reads On   Asks for Help   Repeats   Attempts to Self-Correct

"Sounds Out" (Segmenting)   Blends Sounds   Structural Analysis (Root words, Affixes)

C. Cueing Systems Used in Attempting Words

CUEING TOOL	MISCUE EXAMPLES	ACTUAL TEXT
(M) Meaning		
(S) Syntax		
(V) Visual		

D. Fluency (word by word → fluent reading)

Word by Word _____   Mixed Phrasing _____   Fluent Reading _____   Fluency Rate in Seconds _____

Performance Summary

Silent Reading Comprehension

_____ 0–1 questions missed = Easy

_____ 2 questions missed = Adequate

_____ 3+ questions missed = Too hard

Oral Reading Accuracy

_____ 0–1 oral error = Easy

_____ 2–5 oral errors = Adequate

_____ 6+ oral errors = Too hard

Continue to the next reading passage? _____ Yes   _____ No

PART IV: LISTENING COMPREHENSION

Directions: If you have decided not to continue to have the student read any other passages, then use this passage to begin assessing the student's listening comprehension (see page 19). Begin by reading the background statement for this passage and then say, "I am going to read this story to you. Please listen carefully because I will be asking you some questions after I finish reading it to you." After reading the passage, ask the student the questions associated with the passage. If the student correctly answers more than six questions, you will need to move to the next level and repeat the procedure.

Listening Comprehension

_____ 0–2 questions missed = move to the next passage level

_____ more than 2 questions missed = stop assessment or move down a level

Examiner's Notes:

LEVEL 5 ASSESSMENT PROTOCOLS

Hot Shoes (324 words)

PART I: SILENT READING COMPREHENSION

Background Statement: "This story is about how one group of boys feel about their athletic shoes. Read this story to find out how important special shoes are to playing sports. Read it carefully because I will ask you to tell me about it when you finish."

Teacher Directions: Once the student completes the silent reading, say, "Tell me about the story you just read." Answers to the questions below that the student provides during the retelling should be marked "ua" in the appropriate blank to indicate that this response was unaided. Ask all remaining questions not addressed during the retelling and mark those the student answers with an "a" to indicate the correct response was given after prompting by the teacher.

Questions/Answers

Story Grammar Element/ Level of Comprehension

_____ 1. Where did the story take place?
(*I. B. Belcher Elementary School or at a school*)

setting/literal

_____ 2. Who were the two main characters in the story?
(*Jamie Lee and Josh Kidder*)

character-characterization/literal

_____ 3. What was the problem between Jamie and Josh?
(*Jamie didn't think Josh could be a good player because of his shoes, Josh didn't fit in, or other plausible responses*)

story problem(s)/inferential

_____ 4. How did Josh solve his problem with the other boys?
(*he outplayed all of them*)

problem resolution/inferential

_____ 5. What kind of person was Jamie Lee?
(*conceited, stuck-up, or other plausible responses*)

character-characterization/evaluative

_____ 6. What happened after the game?
(*the other boys gathered around and asked Josh his secret*)

problem resolution attempts/literal

_____ 7. Why did everyone laugh when Josh said, "Two things—lots of practice and cheap shoes"?
(*because everything had happened because of his cheap shoes*)

problem resolution attempts/inferential

_____ 8. What lesson does this story teach?
(*responses will vary but should indicate a theme/ moral related to "it's not what you wear that makes you good in a sport"*)

theme/evaluative

PART II: ORAL READING AND ANALYSIS OF MISCUES

Directions: Say, "Now I would like to hear you read this story out loud." Have the student read orally until the 100-word sample is completed. Follow along on the Miscue Grid, marking any oral reading errors as appropriate. *Remember to count miscues only up to the point in the story containing the oral reading stop-marker (///).* Then complete the Developmental/Performance Summary to determine whether to continue the assessment. (*Note:* The Miscue Grid should be completed *after* the assessment session has been concluded in order to minimize stress for the student.)

ERROR TYPES / ERROR ANALYSIS

	mis-pronun.	sub-stitute	inser-tions	tchr. assist	omis-sions	Error Totals	Self-Correct.	(M) Meaning	(S) Syntax	(V) Visual
Hot Shoes										
The guys at the I. B. Belcher										
Elementary School loved all the new sport										
shoes. Some wore the "Sky High"										
model by Leader. Others who										
couldn't afford Sky Highs would settle										
for a lesser shoe. Some liked the "Street										
Smarts" by Master, or the										
"Uptown-Downtown" by Beebop.										
The Belcher boys got to the point										
with their shoes that they could										
identify their friends just by										
looking at their feet. But the boy who										
was the envy of the entire fifth										
grade was Jamie Lee. He had a										
pair of "High Five Pump'em Ups"										
by Superior. The only thing Belcher										
boys // *loved as much as their*										
shoes was basketball.										
TOTALS										

Summary of Reading Behaviors (Strengths and Needs)

PART III: MISCUE ANALYSIS

Directions: *Circle all reading behaviors you observed.*

A. Fundamental Behaviors Observed:

L → R Directionality   1 to 1 Matching   Searching for Clues   Cross-Checking

B. Word Attack Behaviors:

No Attempt   Mispronunciation (Invented word)   Substitutes

Skips/Reads On   Asks for Help   Repeats   Attempts to Self-Correct

"Sounds Out" (Segmenting)   Blends Sounds   Structural Analysis (Root words, Affixes)

C. Cueing Systems Used in Attempting Words

CUEING TOOL	MISCUE EXAMPLES	ACTUAL TEXT
(M) Meaning		
(S) Syntax		
(V) Visual		

D. Fluency (word by word → fluent reading)

Word by Word _____   Mixed Phrasing _____   Fluent Reading _____   Fluency Rate in Seconds _____

Performance Summary

Silent Reading Comprehension

_____ 0–1 questions missed = Easy

_____ 2 questions missed = Adequate

_____ 3+ questions missed = Too hard

Oral Reading Accuracy

_____ 0–1 oral error = Easy

_____ 2–5 oral errors = Adequate

_____ 6+ oral errors = Too hard

Continue to the next reading passage? _____ Yes   _____ No

PART IV: LISTENING COMPREHENSION

Directions: If you have decided not to continue to have the student read any other passages, then use this passage to begin assessing the student's listening comprehension (see page 19). Begin by reading the background statement for this passage and then say, "I am going to read this story to you. Please listen carefully because I will be asking you some questions after I finish reading it to you." After reading the passage, ask the student the questions associated with the passage. If the student correctly answers more than six questions, you will need to move to the next level and repeat the procedure.

Listening Comprehension

_____ 0–2 questions missed = move to the next passage level

_____ more than 2 questions missed = stop assessment or move down a level

Examiner's Notes:

LEVEL 6 ASSESSMENT PROTOCOLS

Mountain Fire (367 words)

PART I: SILENT READING COMPREHENSION

Background Statement: "This story is about two boys who are lost on a mountain. Read the story to find out what they did to find their way home and what were the results of their problem resolution attempts. Read it carefully because I will ask you to tell me about what you read."

Teacher Directions: Once the student completes the silent reading, say, "Tell me about the story you just read." Answers to the questions below that the student provides during the retelling should be marked "ua" in the appropriate blank to indicate that this response was unaided. Ask all remaining questions not addressed during the retelling and mark those the student answers with an "a" to indicate that the correct response was given after prompting by the teacher.

Questions/Answers	*Story Grammar Element/ Level of Comprehension*
_____ 1. Where did the story take place? (*Mount Holyoak*)	setting/literal
_____ 2. Who were the two boys in the story? (*Brad, Kevin*)	character-characterization/literal
_____ 3. Why were the boys sent upstream by Brad's father? (*to look for cougar tracks*)	problem resolution attempts/inferential
_____ 4. What was Brad's and Kevin's problem after going upstream? (*they became lost*)	story problem(s)/literal
_____ 5. What did the boys do to be found? (*they started a fire*)	problem resolution/literal
_____ 6. What happened after their fire got out of hand? (*people came and put the fire out; other specifics related to this question are acceptable*)	problem resolution attempts/literal
_____ 7. After the forest fire was put out, what did the boys do? (*helped reforest the area*)	problem resolution attempts/literal
_____ 8. What new problem resulted from the forest fire? (*cougars were no longer in the area*)	story problem(s)/inferential

PART II: ORAL READING AND ANALYSIS OF MISCUES

Directions: Say, "Now I would like to hear you read this story out loud." Have the student read orally until the 100-word sample is completed. Follow along on the Miscue Grid, marking any oral reading errors as appropriate. *Remember to count miscues only up to the point in the story containing the oral reading stop-marker (///).* Then complete the Developmental/Performance Summary to determine whether to continue the assessment. (*Note:* The Miscue Grid should be completed *after* the assessment session has been concluded in order to minimize stress for the student.)

	ERROR TYPES							ERROR ANALYSIS		
	mis-pronun.	sub-stitute	inser-tions	tchr. assist	omis-sions	Error Totals	Self-Correct.	(M) Meaning	(S) Syntax	(V) Visual
Mountain Fire										
One August afternoon Brad and Kevin										
went tracking with their fathers on										
Mount Holyoak. Brad's father was a										
conservationist for the Forest Service										
and was searching for evidence of										
cougars. Many people feared that the										
cougars were extinct on Mount Holyoak.										
The boys became excited when they										
found what appeared to be a partial										
cougar track near a stream. But as										
the day wore on, no new tracks were										
found. After lunch Brad's father sent										
the boys upstream while he circled										
west. He told the boys to return to the lunch site										
in an hour. After about forty-five minutes,//										
the boys found the stream's										
source and could follow it no more.										
TOTALS										

Summary of Reading Behaviors (Strengths and Needs)

PART III: MISCUE ANALYSIS

Directions: *Circle all reading behaviors you observed.*

A. Fundamental Behaviors Observed:

L → R Directionality   1 to 1 Matching   Searching for Clues   Cross-Checking

B. Word Attack Behaviors:

No Attempt   Mispronunciation (Invented word)   Substitutes

Skips/Reads On   Asks for Help   Repeats   Attempts to Self-Correct

"Sounds Out" (Segmenting)   Blends Sounds   Structural Analysis (Root words, Affixes)

C. Cueing Systems Used in Attempting Words

CUEING TOOL	MISCUE EXAMPLES	ACTUAL TEXT
(M) Meaning		
(S) Syntax		
(V) Visual		

D. Fluency (word by word → fluent reading)

Word by Word _____   Mixed Phrasing _____   Fluent Reading _____   Fluency Rate in Seconds _____

Performance Summary

Silent Reading Comprehension

_____ 0–1 questions missed = Easy

_____ 2 questions missed = Adequate

_____ 3+ questions missed = Too hard

Oral Reading Accuracy

_____ 0–1 oral error = Easy

_____ 2–5 oral errors = Adequate

_____ 6+ oral errors = Too hard

Continue to the next reading passage? _____ Yes   _____ No

PART IV: LISTENING COMPREHENSION

Directions: If you have decided not to continue to have the student read any other passages, then use this passage to begin assessing the student's listening comprehension (see page 19). Begin by reading the background statement for this passage and then say, "I am going to read this story to you. Please listen carefully because I will be asking you some questions after I finish reading it to you." After reading the passage, ask the student the questions associated with the passage. If the student correctly answers more than six questions, you will need to move to the next level and repeat the procedure.

Listening Comprehension

_____ 0–2 questions missed = move to the next passage level

_____ more than 2 questions missed = stop assessment or move down a level

Examiner's Notes:

LEVEL 7 ASSESSMENT PROTOCOLS

The Canoe Trip (490 words)

PART I: SILENT READING COMPREHENSION

Background Statement: "The story is about two girls who take a canoe trip. Read the story and find out what happens to the girls while canoeing. Read it carefully because I'm going to ask you to tell me about it when you finish."

Teacher Directions: Once the student completes the silent reading, say, "Tell me about the story you just read." Answers to the questions below that the student provides during the retelling should be marked "ua" in the appropriate blank to indicate that this response was unaided. Ask all remaining questions not addressed during the retelling and mark those the student answers with an "a" to indicate that the correct response was given after prompting by the teacher.

Questions/Answers

Story Grammar Element/ Level of Comprehension

_____ 1. Where did this story take place?
(*West Yellowstone*)

setting/literal

_____ 2. Who was the story mainly about?
(*Katherine and Amy*)

character-characterization/literal

_____ 3. What was the girls' problem?
(*they capsized their canoe*)

story problem(s)/literal

_____ 4. What happened after they capsized?
(*they lost their food but saved the canoe*)

problem resolution attempts/inferential

_____ 5. Why couldn't the girls catch up with the floating coolers?
(*because of the time it took to empty the canoe and the swiftness of the water*)

problem resolution attempts/inferential

_____ 6. How did the problem of the lost food turn out?
(*Katherine's parents caught the floating coolers*)

story solution/literal

_____ 7. How did Katherine and Amy feel after reaching Katherine's parents?
(*relieved, embarrassed, or other plausible responses*)

character-characterization/evaluative

_____ 8. Why is "all's well that ends well" a good theme for this story?
(*responses will vary but should reflect the fact that the girls didn't give up and everything turned out fine when they reached Katherine's parents*)

theme/evaluative

PART II: ORAL READING AND ANALYSIS OF MISCUES

Directions: Say, "Now I would like to hear you read this story out loud." Have the student read orally until the 100-word sample is completed. Follow along on the Miscue Grid, marking any oral reading errors as appropriate. *Remember to count miscues only up to the point in the story containing the oral reading stop-marker (//).* Then complete the Developmental/Performance Summary to determine whether to continue the assessment. (*Note:* The Miscue Grid should be completed *after* the assessment session has been concluded in order to minimize stress for the student.)

ERROR TYPES | **ERROR ANALYSIS**

The Canoe Trip	mis-pronun.	sub-stitute	inser-tions	tchr. assist	omis-sions	Error Totals	Self-Correct.	(M) Meaning	(S) Syntax	(V) Visual
Katherine and her family like to spend their										
vacation camping out. Frequently they										
go to either Great Smoky										
Mountains National Park or Yellowstone										
National Park. Since they have										
camped out for many years,										
they have become quite accomplished.										
Katherine is able to start a fire with flint										
and steel, build a lean-to for shelter,										
and find food in the forest on which to live.										
Katherine's favorite outdoor activity is canoeing.										
Although she is quite a good canoer, there is										
one canoe trip that she'll never forget.										
It was a canoe trip she took with her family										
and her friend // *Amy down the Madison*										
River near West Yellowstone.										
TOTALS										

Summary of Reading Behaviors (Strengths and Needs)

PART III: MISCUE ANALYSIS

Directions: *Circle all reading behaviors you observed.*

A. Fundamental Behaviors Observed:

L → R Directionality   1 to 1 Matching   Searching for Clues   Cross-Checking

B. Word Attack Behaviors:

No Attempt   Mispronunciation (Invented word)   Substitutes

Skips/Reads On   Asks for Help   Repeats   Attempts to Self-Correct

"Sounds Out" (Segmenting)   Blends Sounds   Structural Analysis (Root words, Affixes)

C. Cueing Systems Used in Attempting Words

CUEING TOOL	MISCUE EXAMPLES	ACTUAL TEXT
(M) Meaning		
(S) Syntax		
(V) Visual		

D. Fluency (word by word → fluent reading)

Word by Word _____   Mixed Phrasing _____   Fluent Reading _____   Fluency Rate in Seconds _____

Performance Summary

Silent Reading Comprehension

_____ 0–1 questions missed = Easy

_____ 2 questions missed = Adequate

_____ 3+ questions missed = Too hard

Oral Reading Accuracy

_____ 0–1 oral error = Easy

_____ 2–5 oral errors = Adequate

_____ 6+ oral errors = Too hard

Continue to the next reading passage? _____ Yes   _____ No

PART IV: LISTENING COMPREHENSION

Directions: If you have decided not to continue to have the student read any other passages, then use this passage to begin assessing the student's listening comprehension (see page 19). Begin by reading the background statement for this passage and then say, "I am going to read this story to you. Please listen carefully because I will be asking you some questions after I finish reading it to you." After reading the passage, ask the student the questions associated with the passage. If the student correctly answers more than six questions, you will need to move to the next level and repeat the procedure.

Listening Comprehension

_____ 0–2 questions missed = move to the next passage level

_____ more than 2 questions missed = stop assessment or move down a level

Examiner's Notes:

FORM A LEVEL 8 ASSESSMENT PROTOCOLS

The Eagle (504 words)

PART I: SILENT READING COMPREHENSION

Background Statement: "This story is an old Native American tale about an eagle. Read the passage and try to identify the message the story tells. Read it carefully because I'm going to ask you to tell me about it when you finish."

Teacher Directions: Once the student completes the silent reading, say, "Tell me about the story you just read." Answers to the questions below that the student provides during the retelling should be marked "ua" in the appropriate blank to indicate that this response was unaided. Ask all remaining questions not addressed during the retelling and mark those the student answers with an "a" to indicate that the correct response was given after prompting by the teacher.

Questions/Answers	*Story Grammar Element/ Level of Comprehension*
_____ 1. Where does the story take place? (*mountain and farm*)	setting/literal
_____ 2. Who were the people in the story? (*Hopi farmer, his son, and Anasazi brave*)	character-characterization/literal
_____ 3. What was the problem presented in the story? (*convincing the eagle that he wasn't a chicken*)	story problem(s)/inferential
_____ 4. What did the eagle do that was like a chicken? (*scratching, pecking at food, wouldn't fly*)	problem resolution attempts/literal
_____ 5. What was the brave's first attempt to convince the bird it was an eagle? (*tried to get it to fly from barn*)	problem resolution attempts/literal
_____ 6. How did the brave finally get the bird to recognize it could fly? (*by taking it up to a high bluff so that it could see the valley and sense freedom*)	problem resolution/literal
_____ 7. What words would you use to describe the farmer? (*responses will vary but should relate to the farmer being deceitful, uncaring, or a liar*)	character-characterization/evaluative
_____ 8. What lesson does this story teach? (*responses will vary but should indicate a theme/ moral related to "you are what you think you are"*)	theme/evaluative

PART II: ORAL READING AND ANALYSIS OF MISCUES

Directions: Say, "Now I would like to hear you read this story out loud." Have the student read orally until the 100-word sample is completed. Follow along on the Miscue Grid, marking any oral reading errors as appropriate. *Remember to count miscues only up to the point in the story containing the oral reading stop-marker (///).* Then complete the Developmental/Performance Summary to determine whether to continue the assessment. (*Note:* The Miscue Grid should be completed *after* the assessment session has been concluded in order to minimize stress for the student.)

ERROR TYPES

ERROR ANALYSIS

The Eagle	mis-pronun.	sub-stitute	inser-tions	tchr. assist	omis-sions	Error Totals	Self-Correct.	(M) Meaning	(S) Syntax	(V) Visual
There exists an old Native American legend										
about an eagle who thought he was a										
chicken. It seems that a Hopi farmer										
and his only son decided to climb										
a nearby mountain										
to observe an										
eagle's nest. The trip would take them all day,										
so they brought along some rations and water										
for the trek. The man and the boy crossed the										
enormous fields of maize and beans										
into the foothills. Soon thereafter										
they were ascending the mountain,										
and the climb became rigorous										
and hazardous. They occasionally										
looked back toward their home and										
at the panoramic view of the entire //										
valley. Finally the farmer and son										
reached the mountain's summit.										
TOTALS										

Summary of Reading Behaviors (Strengths and Needs)

PART III: MISCUE ANALYSIS

Directions: *Circle all reading behaviors you observed.*

A. Fundamental Behaviors Observed:

L → R Directionality   1 to 1 Matching   Searching for Clues   Cross-Checking

B. Word Attack Behaviors:

No Attempt   Mispronunciation (Invented word)   Substitutes

Skips/Reads On   Asks for Help   Repeats   Attempts to Self-Correct

"Sounds Out" (Segmenting)   Blends Sounds   Structural Analysis (Root words, Affixes)

C. Cueing Systems Used in Attempting Words

CUEING TOOL	MISCUE EXAMPLES	ACTUAL TEXT
(M) Meaning		
(S) Syntax		
(V) Visual		

D. Fluency (word by word → fluent reading)

Word by Word _____   Mixed Phrasing _____   Fluent Reading _____   Fluency Rate in Seconds _____

Performance Summary

Silent Reading Comprehension

_____ 0–1 questions missed = Easy

_____ 2 questions missed = Adequate

_____ 3+ questions missed = Too hard

Oral Reading Accuracy

_____ 0–1 oral error = Easy

_____ 2–5 oral errors = Adequate

_____ 6+ oral errors = Too hard

Continue to the next reading passage? _____ Yes   _____ No

PART IV: LISTENING COMPREHENSION

Directions: If you have decided not to continue to have the student read any other passages, then use this passage to begin assessing the student's listening comprehension (see page 19). Begin by reading the background statement for this passage and then say, "I am going to read this story to you. Please listen carefully because I will be asking you some questions after I finish reading it to you." After reading the passage, ask the student the questions associated with the passage. If the student correctly answers more than six questions, you will need to move to the next level and repeat the procedure.

Listening Comprehension

_____ 0–2 questions missed = move to the next passage level

_____ more than 2 questions missed = stop assessment or move down a level

Examiner's Notes:

A LEVEL 9 ASSESSMENT PROTOCOLS

The Case of Angela Violet (378 words)

PART I: SILENT READING COMPREHENSION

Background Statement: "This story is about a young girl's disappearance. Read the story carefully because I will ask you to tell it to me when you finish."

Teacher Directions: Once the student completes the silent reading, say, "Tell me about the story you just read." Answers to the questions below that the student provides during the retelling should be marked "ua" in the appropriate blank to indicate that this response was unaided. Ask all remaining questions not addressed during the retelling and mark those the student answers with an "a" to indicate that the correct response was given after prompting by the teacher.

Questions/Answers	*Story Grammar Element/ Level of Comprehension*
_____ 1. What time of year did the story take place? *(autumn)*	setting/literal
_____ 2. What was the main problem in the story? *(Katrina Bowers had disappeared)*	story problem(s)/inferential
_____ 3. What problem resolution attempts did the authorities take when they received the telephone tip? *(they got a search warrant and went to Miss Violet's house)*	problem resolution attempts/literal
_____ 4. How was Katrina's case finally solved? *(she was found in California)*	problem resolution/literal
_____ 5. What was Miss Violet's reaction to the police wanting to search her house? *(she didn't mind, she welcomed the search)*	problem resolution attempts/literal
_____ 6. What kind of person was Miss Violet? *(responses will vary but should suggest kind, caring, gentle, lonely)*	character-characterization/inferential
_____ 7. What did the people in the community do after Miss Violet was proved innocent? *(began to do things for and with her)*	problem resolution attempts/literal
_____ 8. What is the lesson of this story? *(responses will vary but should indicate a theme/ moral related to "you can't judge a book by its cover")*	theme/evaluative

PART II: ORAL READING AND ANALYSIS OF MISCUES

Directions: Say, "Now I would like to hear you read this story out loud." Have the student read orally until the 100-word sample is completed. Follow along on the Miscue Grid, marking any oral reading errors as appropriate. *Remember to count miscues only up to the point in the story containing the oral reading stop-marker (///).* Then complete the Developmental/Performance Summary to determine whether to continue the assessment. (*Note:* The Miscue Grid should be completed *after* the assessment session has been concluded in order to minimize stress for the student.)

ERROR ANALYSIS

ERROR TYPES

	mis-pronun.	sub-stitute	inser-tions	tchr. assist	omis-sions	Error Totals	Self-Correct.	(M) Meaning	(S) Syntax	(V) Visual
The Case of Angela Violet										
Angela Violet was an elderly lady in our										
neighborhood who some people thought										
suspicious. She was rarely seen outside her										
spacious Victorian-styled home, and then only										
to retrieve the daily mail. Her pasty complexion										
and ancient dress made her appear like an										
apparition. Small children in the neighborhood										
speculated that she might be some sort of witch.										
It appeared that Miss Violet had no contact with										
the outside world. One autumn day news spread										
through the community that a high school										
cheerleader, Katrina Bowers, had disappeared.										
It was feared by the police that Katrina had been										
abducted. State and // local police joined forces										
with the Federal Bureau of Investigation in the										
massive search effort.										
TOTALS										

Summary of Reading Behaviors (Strengths and Needs)

PART III: MISCUE ANALYSIS

Directions: Circle all reading behaviors you observed.

A. Fundamental Behaviors Observed:

L → R Directionality   1 to 1 Matching   Searching for Clues   Cross-Checking

B. Word Attack Behaviors:

No Attempt   Mispronunciation (Invented word)   Substitutes

Skips/Reads On   Asks for Help   Repeats   Attempts to Self-Correct

"Sounds Out" (Segmenting)   Blends Sounds   Structural Analysis (Root words, Affixes)

C. Cueing Systems Used in Attempting Words

CUEING TOOL	MISCUE EXAMPLES	ACTUAL TEXT
(M) Meaning		
(S) Syntax		
(V) Visual		

D. Fluency (word by word → fluent reading)

Word by Word _____   Mixed Phrasing _____   Fluent Reading _____   Fluency Rate in Seconds _____

Performance Summary

Silent Reading Comprehension

_____ 0–1 questions missed = Easy

_____ 2 questions missed = Adequate

_____ 3+ questions missed = Too hard

Oral Reading Accuracy

_____ 0–1 oral error = Easy

_____ 2–5 oral errors = Adequate

_____ 6+ oral errors = Too hard

Continue to the next passage? _____ Yes   _____ No

PART IV: LISTENING COMPREHENSION

Directions: If you have decided not to continue to have the student read any other passages, then use this passage to begin assessing the student's listening comprehension (see page 19). Begin by reading the background statement for this passage and then say, "I am going to read this story to you. Please listen carefully because I will be asking you some questions after I finish reading it to you." After reading the passage, ask the student the questions associated with the passage. If the student correctly answers more than six questions, you will need to move to the next level and repeat the procedure.

Listening Comprehension

_____ 0–2 questions missed = move to the next passage level

_____ more than 2 questions missed = stop assessment or move down a level

Examiner's Notes:

SENTENCES FOR INITIAL PASSAGE SELECTION

FORM B: LEVEL 1

1. Today is my birthday.

2. I wanted to have a party.

3. She stopped at the trees.

FORM B: LEVEL 2

1. We have extra leaves to rake.

2. I need some extra money.

3. She heard me in the kitchen.

FORM B: LEVEL 3

1. I was beginning to get afraid.

2. He could hear the voice get closer.

3. Tomorrow I will finish my work.

FORM B: LEVEL 4

1. She walked carefully into the darkness.

2. I know it is important to eat vegetables.

3. He slipped as he reached up into the oak tree.

FORM B: LEVEL 5

1. The tree withered away after the storm.

2. The neighborhood was shaken after the fire.

3. I was frightened by my dream.

FORM B: LEVEL 6

1. By not participating, he was barely passing in school.

2. I allowed the gifted students extra time.

3. Especially high achievement is a result of good instruction.

FORM B: LEVEL 7

1. I made an appointment to purchase the bike.

2. The plastic covering the application form was especially thick.

3. His robust legs made a difference in his overall physical strength.

FORM B: LEVEL 8

1. He was provoked because he was small in stature.

2. The familiar mockery led to the fight.

3. His bruised ego never really recovered.

FORM B: LEVEL 9

1. Her nontraditional dress improved her appearance.

2. The anonymous letter wasn't taken seriously.

3. He was a formidable-looking person, even wearing a sleazy coat.

FORM

NARRATIVE PASSAGES

Eyes in My Closet

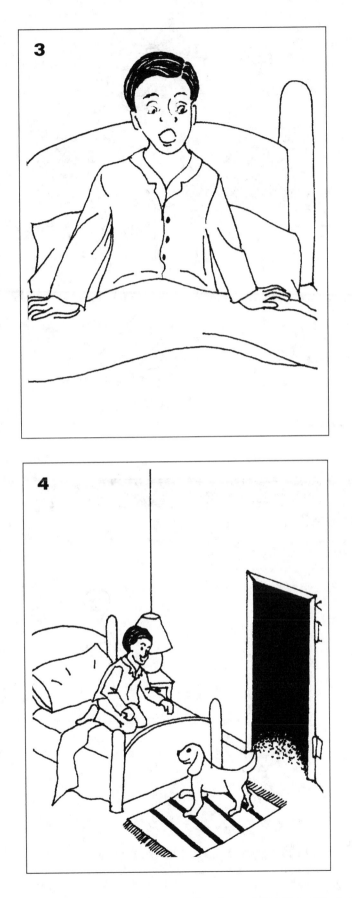

The T-Ball Game

I like to play T-ball at school.

On Friday we played the big game.

3

I got a hit at the end of the game.

4

I made it home and won the game.

Birthday at the Zoo

It was Sunday.

I got out of bed and went to eat.

Mom said, "Today is your birthday, Pat. What do you want to do?"

I wanted a party but I did not tell Mom.

I said, "I just want to play."

Mom said, "Come take a ride with me."

I got in the car and soon we were in the city.

The car stopped. We got out.

We walked past some trees and I saw a sign that said "City Zoo."

All my friends were at the gate.

I was all smiles. Mom had planned a party for me.

It was the best birthday ever.

Mary's New Bike

Mary wanted a new bike. She helped around the house to make money. She had even helped her father rake leaves for extra money. But she still didn't have the money for the new ten-speed bike.

One day her Aunt Deb came to visit Mary's family. Aunt Deb heard that Mary wanted a new bike. She told Mary that she had some work for her. Mary walked over to Aunt Deb's house the very next day.

Aunt Deb had Mary mop her kitchen floor. Mary cleaned out the flower beds. Mary swept out the carport. Finally Aunt Deb asked Mary to fold her clean clothes. Mary was tired by the end of the day. But when Aunt Deb paid Mary her money, Mary smiled and hugged Aunt Deb. She hurried home to tell her parents the good news. They smiled and told her how proud they were.

The next day Mary went to the store.

Bedtime

The sun was going down. The air was hot and Wild Willie was afraid. Never had he been in such a dry, hot place. His horse, Wizard was trying to find a few blades of grass. Wild Willie was beginning fall asleep from staying awake so long. Then he heard the sound again—the same sound he had been hearing for days. What could be? Why was it following him? How could he find out what or whe it was?

Slowly Wizard turned around. Willie stood up in the stirrups to s over the sand dune. He saw no one. Again he heard the sound. Th time it came from behind. It was a slow rumbling sound. He got c his horse. He took his gun and got ready. Slowly the sound came closer and closer. Willie raised his gun. . . .

Then the TV went off and a voice said, "Beth, it's time to go tc bed. Tomorrow is a school day and it's getting late." "Aw, Mom, can't I finish seeing the show?" I asked. "No, you can watch it another time," my mother replied.

As I went slowly upstairs to bed, I wondered what Wild Willie had seen. Maybe it had been some kind of animal or just a person in a wagon. But it was probably the Ghost of the Sand Wind. Yeah, that had to be it. Other people had claimed to have seen it. But I won't know until the reruns.

A Different Time

Marlo lived in a different time and a different place. He lived in a time of darkness and gloom. Marlo lived in a small hut with his poor parents. He didn't have nice clothes and he didn't have much to eat. But neither of these things bothered Marlo. There was only one thing he wanted. But he couldn't have it because the ruler would not let any of his people have it. This most important thing was to be able to read. Today this may seem like a dumb wish, but to Marlo it wasn't.

One day Marlo's father sent him to the castle with a cart of vegetables. On the way Marlo met an old man who had strange eyes. The old man's head was hooded, but his eyes were deep blue and sparkled. The old man asked Marlo if he could please have a few vegetables to eat. Marlo agreed even though he knew he would get into trouble. When the old man finished, he said, "Come to the old oak tree tonight and the future will be yours." Marlo walked away wondering what the old man meant.

That night Marlo slipped out of the hut. He ran up the road until he reached the old oak tree. There he found the old man sitting on the ground.

The old man stood up and handed Marlo a box. He said, "Marlo, inside this box is what you want. Your life will never be the same."

Marlo took the box, looked down for a second, and then the old man was nowhere to be seen. Marlo rushed home. He carefully opened the box. And there in the light of his one candle Marlo saw what was in the box. It was a book.

Afternoon Walk

One day Allison was walking in the woods behind her house. Some of the other children in the neighborhood liked to tease her by saying that the woods were haunted. "There's an old, withered, witch-like woman in those woods who comes out at two o'clock every day to catch children," they'd say. "She makes them do housework and things like that. Then she sells them to a grim looking dwarf from far away when they are too tired to work. Once captured they are never seen again." Allison knew her friends were only telling stories, but it still frightened her sometimes when she went into the woods.

On this particular morning, Allison thought she would take a short stroll to find wild flowers for her mother. After walking for an hour or so, she stopped to rest under an elm tree. Unfortunately she fell fast asleep. The next thing she knew, Allison was being shaken by a terribly ugly old woman dressed all in black. Startled, Allison looked at her watch. It was two o'clock. The old woman took Allison to a run-down old hut.

For what seemed like hours, Allison had to wash dishes, clean out a doghouse, and scrub floors. While cleaning out the doghouse, she found a dog tag that read "Spirit." She tucked it into her pocket thinking she would give it to the woman later. The old woman checked on Allison every few minutes. She always asked Allison if she were tired. Allison always said that she wasn't tired because she remembered the story of the dwarf.

It was just after Allison finished the doghouse that her chance to escape occurred. The old woman went into a back room calling for Spirit so Allison quickly ran out the door. Allison ran and ran until she finally couldn't run any farther. She lay down under an elm tree and fell asleep.

Allison was awakened by her brother who said, "Mom says it's getting late and you'd better come home quick." Allison said. "Oh, boy, what an awful dream I just had." She told her brother all about her dream on the way home. All he said was, "Get serious."

That night when Allison undressed to take her bath, a small metal tag fell from her pocket that had "Spirit" printed on it.

Laser Boy

My name is Bob and I'm a teacher. Several years ago I knew a student that I'd like to tell you about.

Matthew was a 13-year-old who never seemed to do well in school. Some say that he was a misfit, someone who doesn't quite fit in with the other kids his age. Not only that, Matthew had trouble in school nearly his whole life. He failed to complete his homework even when it was an easy assignment. By not participating in class, not turning in homework, and only doing a fair job on tests, Matthew always seemed to be just barely passing.

One day when Matthew was in seventh grade, his teacher decided to find out what Matthew's problem was in school. The teacher had him tested and found out from the special education teacher that Matthew was gifted in the areas of science and mathematics! The special education teacher said, "Oh, yes, sometimes students who do poorly in school are quite gifted. They just haven't been allowed to show what they can do. Also, some gifted students are not especially strong in some school subjects. But they are excellent in music, working with mechanical objects, or even athletics."

After Matthew's discovery was made, he was asked what he was interested in studying. Matthew answered that he wanted to study lasers. For the rest of that year, Matthew read everything he could find in the library at the university having to do with lasers. Later, a professor in California was found who was an expert on laser technology. The professor agreed to talk with Matthew on a regular basis to help answer questions or solve any problems Matthew had.

During the last part of seventh grade, Matthew worked on a special science project. He built a model laser. It was fantastic! Matthew's model was accurate to the last detail. Everyone was very impressed with his project. All the kids at school began calling him "laser boy." He found new friends and his life at school and home greatly improved.

Since that very special year when I got to know "laser boy," I've looked at students who are experiencing trouble in a new way. I'm convinced that everyone has special talents. We only need to discover what they are.

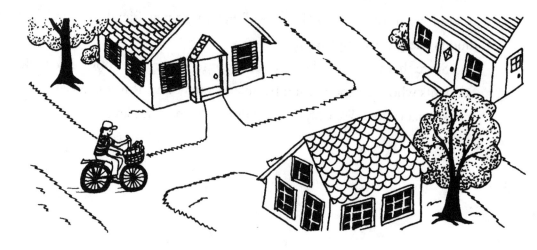

The Paper Route

Scott had a chance to earn his own money for the first time. Answering an advertisement for newspaper carriers, he set up an appointment with Mr. Miley, the distribution manager. Mr. Miley was a rather short and stocky man who spoke with a loud voice.

After reviewing Scott's application, Mr. Miley said, "You look like a dependable young man to me. Do your parents approve of your becoming a paperboy?" "Yes, sir," replied Scott, "and I have a letter from my Dad saying it's OK with him."

"You can have the job, Scott," said Mr. Miley. "However, I want you to realize that this is a long route and you will have to get up very early. You will also have to have robust legs and a good bike," warned Mr. Miley.

Getting started was not easy. Scott had to be out of bed by 4:30 a.m. Next he had to pick up the papers and roll them up for placement in a plastic bag. He would usually finish that much by 5:30 a.m. Then it was time to deliver the papers.

Most days Scott could deliver all his newspapers in just two trips. His father had purchased a new bike for Scott and attached an enormous basket to it. The really hard days were Thursday and Sunday. Newspapers were especially large on those days. Scott would have to make as many as five trips to get the papers delivered on those days.

The good part of the job was, of course, the money. Scott found that he was making about 250 dollars a month. He was also developing his physical strength.

But the negative side of the job was bad weather and cranky customers. When it rained, Scott got drenched. When it snowed, Scott froze. Scott's biggest complaint was his cranky customers, particularly Mr. Gripper. Mr. Gripper insisted on his paper being put in his mailbox, rain or shine. If Scott failed to do this, Mr. Gripper always called the newspaper office and complained. But Scott avoided most complaints by going out of his way to please his customers.

After one year on the job, Scott was called into Mr. Miley's office for an end-of-year conference. During the year Scott had managed to save 1,300 dollars and pay back his father for the bike. So when Mr. Miley asked him if he wanted to continue working for the paper, Scott said, "Yes." But he added, "It was a lot more work than I counted on and I could live without the Mr. Grippers of the world. But I really like the work."

Riley and Leonard

At times Leonard felt like the most unpopular boy in school. No matter what he did, he was constantly ridiculed by his classmates. Maybe it was because he was small in stature and wore thick bifocals. Or maybe it was because he didn't like sports. Possibly it was because he couldn't afford the designer clothes the other kids seemed to live for. Regardless, Leonard felt like a loser and was unhappy with his situation.

One day, while putting his books in his locker, the familiar mockery began. A small covey of classmates formed a semicircle around Leonard. Each began to taunt him and call him names. Most joined in after Riley McClure made Leonard drop his books. They all laughed and called him *bozo, nerd,* and *dweeb.* But Leonard tried not to be provoked—that is, until Riley made horrible slurs about Leonard's family and particularly Leonard's mother. Leonard couldn't resist. He lunged at Riley but Riley was much bigger and Leonard's attack ended in disaster. Riley slammed him into the lockers, grabbed Leonard by the throat, and made Leonard holler "calf rope," a sign of total submission.

As the group disbanded, so they wouldn't be late for their next class, Lorrie Warner approached Leonard. She apologized for the group's behavior and tried to comfort Leonard's hurt pride. She said, "What goes around comes around." But her consoling didn't help Leonard's bruised ego.

Twenty years later Leonard found himself president of the largest bank in town. He was well respected in the community and was quite generous when it came to civic projects. Although he had never married, he had recently begun dating Lorrie Warner, his old classmate.

One Friday evening Leonard and Lorrie were eating at a fancy restaurant. They had finished their meal and were heading out the door when a beggar approached. The beggar requested money to buy food. There was something curious about the beggar that Leonard could not place. But being generous, Leonard gave the man ten dollars. The beggar was so surprised by the large amount that he shook Leonard's hand vigorously before quickly backing away into the street. Lorrie screamed a word of caution but it was too late. The beggar had stepped into the path of a truck and was struck broadside. Leonard and Lorrie waited for the ambulance to carry the man away.

The next morning the headlines carried the story of the beggar. He had died from internal injuries early that morning. As Leonard read the details, he suddenly dropped the paper and turned pale. The beggar's name was Riley McClure.

The Long Night

I arrived late at the New Orleans International Airport because of delays in St. Louis. The night was descending on the Crescent City as I entered the cab for the short ride to city center. As the cab headed toward the city, the cabbie engaged me in an informative conversation about the Crescent City. She had an island accent and her multicolored dress was very nontraditional. After I told her I wanted to go to Rampart in the French Quarter, she abruptly turned left and headed southwest.

Fifteen minutes later, without a word, I got out of the cab and proceeded up Rampart. I had gone only two blocks when I noticed that a bleak little man was following me. I say bleak because when I saw his silhouette under a fluorescent street light, he looked as if something mean and cruel had happened in his early life. You know, he had a kind of woebegone appearance. Every time I stopped, he stopped. If I sped up my pace, his pace quickened. Finally, I slipped into an anonymous doorway. As he approached I swiftly reached out and grabbed him by his grimy coat. I asked him why he was following me but all he did was whimper and hand me a crumpled-up note. As my eyes fell on the note, he slipped out of my grasp and ran into the eerily approaching fog.

The note contained the following message: "Your death is behind you. Run if you value your life." I didn't think, I ran.

As I rounded the corner of Rampart and Royal, I ran straight into a policeman. I felt relief. I told him my story. He chuckled and didn't take me seriously. As he walked away I saw a set of eyes from behind a refuse container in an alleyway. I ran again.

As I cut through an alley I was accosted by two large, burly men. They said they had been sent by Nero. They asked me where I had put the package. I told them I had no idea of what they were referring to. They gathered me up and forced me into a dingy building.

As soon as my eyes adjusted to the glow of the incandescent lights, I saw a large, rotund man at a table. He looked formidable. I was forced to sit across the table from the man. He leaned forward and I could see his face. A face of evil. He studied me carefully, and then he looked at my assailants. "This isn't Mouser, you idiots. Get him out of here." They blindfolded me and walked me out of the building a different way. An hour later I found myself on a deserted street.

Two days later I left the Crescent City. I never told anyone about my experience, and I've never been back.

EXAMINER'S ASSESSMENT PROTOCOLS

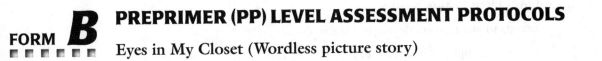
PREPRIMER (PP) LEVEL ASSESSMENT PROTOCOLS

Eyes in My Closet (Wordless picture story)

PART I: WORDLESS PICTURE STORY READING

Background Statement: "These pictures tell a story about a child who is going to bed. Look at each picture as I show it to you and think about the story the pictures tell. Later, I will want you to tell me the story using the pictures."

Teacher Directions: Refer the student to each picture slowly and in order as numbered. Do not comment on the pictures. Then repeat the procedure, asking the student to tell the story in the student's own words. Record the student's reading using a tape recorder, and transcribe the reading as it is being dictated. Replay the recording later to make sure that your transcription is accurate and complete.

PART II: EMERGENT READING BEHAVIOR CHECKLIST

Directions: Following are emergent reading behaviors identified through research and grouped according to broad developmental stages. Check all behaviors you have observed. *If the student progresses to Stage 3 or 4, continue your assessment using the Primer Level (P) passage.*

Stage 1: Early Connections to Reading—Describing Pictures

_____ Attends to and describes (labels) pictures in books

_____ Has a limited sense of story

_____ Follows verbal directions for this activity

_____ Uses oral vocabulary appropriate for age/grade level

_____ Displays attention span appropriate for age/grade level

_____ Responds to questions in an appropriate manner

_____ Appears to connect pictures (sees as being interrelated)

Stage 2: Connecting Pictures to Form a Story

_____ Attends to pictures and develops oral stories.

_____ Uses only childlike or descriptive (storyteller) language to tell the story, rather than book language (i.e., Once upon a time. . . . ; There once was a little boy . . .)

Stage 3: Transitional Picture Reading

_____ Attends to pictures as a connected story

_____ Mixes storyteller language with book language

Stage 4: Advanced Picture Reading

_____ Attends to pictures and develops oral stories

_____ Speaks as though reading the story (uses book language)

Examiner's Notes

PRIMER (P) LEVEL ASSESSMENT PROTOCOLS

The T-Ball Game (32 words)

PART I: PICTURE STORY READING–ORAL READING AND ANALYSIS OF MISCUES

Background Statement: "This is a story about a child who is playing a game. Let's look at each picture first. Now, read the story to yourself. Later, I will want you to read the story to me."

Teacher Directions: Refer the student to each frame of the story slowly and in order as numbered. Do not read the story or comment on the pictures. After the student has read the story silently, ask the student to read the story aloud. Record the student's reading using a tape recorder, and mark any miscues on the Miscue Grid provided. Following the oral reading, complete the Emergent Reading Behavior Checklist. Assessment information obtained from both the Miscue Grid and the Emergent Reading Behavior Checklist will help you to determine whether to continue your assessment. If the student is unable to read the passage independently the first time, read it aloud, then ask the student to try to read the story again. This will help you to understand whether the student is able to memorize and repeat text, an important developmental milestone (see the Instructions for Administering the Preprimer (PP) and Primer (P) Passages section on page 20 for more information). The assessment should stop after this activity, if the child is unable to read the text independently. (*Note:* The Miscue Grid should be completed *after* the assessment session has been concluded in order to minimize stress for the student.)

ERROR TYPES

ERROR ANALYSIS

	mis-pronun.	sub-stitute	inser-tions	tchr. assist	omis-sions	Error Totals	Self-Correct.	(M) Meaning	(S) Syntax	(V) Visual
The T-Ball Game										
I like to play T-ball										
at school. On Friday we										
played the big game. I										
got a hit at the end of										
the game. I made it										
home and won the game.										
TOTALS										

Summary of Reading Behaviors (Strengths and Needs)

PART II: EMERGENT READING BEHAVIOR CHECKLIST

Directions: Following are emergent reading behaviors identified through research and grouped according to broad developmental stages. After the student has completed the oral reading, check each behavior observed below to help determine development level and whether to continue the assessment. *If the student seems to be at Stage 6 or 7 and the oral reading scored at an Easy or Adequate level, continue the assessment using the Level 1 passage.*

Stage 5: Early Print Reading

_____ Tells a story using the pictures

_____ Knows print moves from left to right, top to bottom

_____ Creates part of the text using book language and knows some words on sight

Stage 6: Early Strategic Reading

_____ Uses context to guess at some unknown words (guesses make sense)

_____ Notices beginning sounds in words and uses them in guessing unknown words

_____ Seems to sometimes use syntax to help identify words in print

_____ Recognizes some word parts, such as root words and affixes

Stage 7: Moderate Strategic Reading

_____ Sometimes uses context and word parts to decode words

_____ Self-corrects when making an oral reading miscue

_____ Retells the passage easily and may embellish the story line

_____ Shows some awareness of vowel sounds

Examiner's Notes

PART III: DEVELOPMENTAL/PERFORMANCE SUMMARY

Oral Reading Accuracy

_____ 0–1 oral errors = Easy

_____ 2 oral errors = Adequate

_____ 6+ oral errors = Too hard

Continue to the next assessment level passage? _____ Yes _____ No

Examiner's Notes

LEVEL 1 ASSESSMENT PROTOCOLS

Birthday at the Zoo (106 words)

PART I: SILENT READING COMPREHENSION

Background Statement: "What do you like to do on your birthday? Read this story carefully to find out what special thing a girl wanted for her birthday. I'm going to ask you to tell me about the story when you're through reading it."

Teacher Directions: Once the student completes the silent reading, say, "Tell me about the story you just read." Answers to the questions below that the student provides during the retelling should be marked "ua" in the appropriate blank to indicate that this response was unaided. Ask all remaining questions not addressed during the retelling and mark those the student answers with an "a" to indicate that the correct response was given after prompting by the teacher.

Questions/Answers

Story Grammar Element/ Level of Comprehension

_____ 1. Who were the people in the story?
(*Pat and her Mom*)

character-characterization/literal

_____ 2. What was Pat's wish?
(*Pat wanted to have a party*)

story problem(s)/literal

_____ 3. What did Pat say she wanted to do for her birthday?
(*just play*)

problem resolution attempts/literal

_____ 4. Did Pat get her wish? How do you know?
(*yes, she had a surprise party at the zoo*)

problem resolution/literal

_____ 5. How did Pat and Mom get to the zoo?
(*drove in by car*)

problem resolution attempts/literal

_____ 6. What words would you use to describe how Pat felt at the zoo?
(*surprised, happy, etc.*)

character-characterization/inferential

_____ 7. Where was Pat when the story began?
(*in her bedroom or house*)

setting/inferential

_____ 8. When did Pat first know that she was going to have a birthday party?
(*when she got to the zoo and saw her friends*)

problem resolution attempts/inferential

PART II: ORAL READING AND ANALYSIS OF MISCUES

Directions: Say, "Now I would like to hear you read this story out loud." Have the student read orally until the 100-word sample is completed. Follow along on the Miscue Grid, marking any oral reading errors as appropriate. *Remember to count miscues only up to the point in the story containing the oral reading stop-marker (//).* Then complete the Developmental/Performance Summary to determine whether to continue the assessment. (*Note:* The Miscue Grid should be completed *after* the assessment session has been concluded in order to minimize stress for the student.)

	ERROR TYPES							ERROR ANALYSIS		
Birthday at the Zoo	mis-pronun.	sub-stitute	inser-tions	tchr. assist	omis-sions	Error Totals	Self-Correct.	(M) Meaning	(S) Syntax	(V) Visual
It was Sunday. I got out of bed										
and went to eat. Mom said, "Today										
is your birthday, Pat. What do you										
want to do?" I wanted a party but I										
did not tell Mom. I said, "I just want										
to play." Mom said, "Come take										
a ride with me." I got in the car and										
soon we were in the city. The car										
stopped. We got out. We walked										
past some trees and I saw a sign										
that said "City Zoo." All my friends										
were at the gate. I was all smiles.										
Mom had planned a party for me. //										
It was the best birthday ever.										
TOTALS										

Summary of Reading Behaviors (Strengths and Needs)

PART III: MISCUE ANALYSIS

Directions: *Circle all reading behaviors you observed.*

A. Fundamental Behaviors Observed

L → R Directionality   1 to 1 Matching   Searching for Clues   Cross-Checking

B. Word Attack Behaviors

No Attempt   Mispronunciation (Invented word)   Substitutes

Skips/Reads On   Asks for Help   Repeats   Attempts to Self-Correct

"Sounds Out" (Segmenting)   Blends Sounds   Structural Analysis (Root words, Affixes)

C. Cueing Systems Used in Attempting Words

CUEING TOOL	MISCUE EXAMPLES	ACTUAL TEXT
(M) Meaning		
(S) Syntax		
(V) Visual		

D. Fluency (word by word → fluent reading)

Word by Word _____   Mixed Phrasing _____   Fluent Reading _____   Fluency Rate in Seconds _____

Performance Summary

Silent Reading Comprehension

_____ 0–1 questions missed = Easy

_____ 2 questions missed = Adequate

_____ 3+ questions missed = Too hard

Oral Reading Accuracy

_____ 0–1 oral error = Easy

_____ 2–5 oral errors = Adequate

_____ 6+ oral errors = Too hard

Continue to the next reading passage? _____ Yes   _____ No

PART IV: LISTENING COMPREHENSION

Directions: If you have decided not to continue to have the student read any other passages, then use this passage to begin assessing the student's listening comprehension (see page 19). Begin by reading the background statement for this passage and then say, "I am going to read this story to you. Please listen carefully because I will be asking you some questions after I finish reading it to you." After reading the passage, ask the student the questions associated with the passage. If the student correctly answers more than six questions, you will need to move to the next level and repeat the procedure.

Listening Comprehension

_____ 0–2 questions missed = move to the next passage level

_____ more than 2 questions missed = stop assessment or move down a level

Examiner's Notes:

LEVEL 2 ASSESSMENT PROTOCOLS

Mary's New Bike (156 words)

PART I: SILENT READING COMPREHENSION

Background Statement: "Have you ever tried to earn money for something special? Read this story to find out how Mary was able to earn something special. Read it carefully because I am going to ask you to tell me about the story when you finish."

Teacher Directions: Once the student completes the silent reading, say, "Tell me about the story you just read." Answers to the questions below that the student provides during the retelling should be marked "ua" in the appropriate blank to indicate that this response was unaided. Ask all remaining questions not addressed during the retelling and mark those the student answers with an "a" to indicate that the correct response was given after prompting by the teacher.

Questions/Answers

Story Grammar Element/ Level of Comprehension

_____ 1. Who was this story about?
(*Mary*)

character-characterization/literal

_____ 2. What was Mary's problem in the story?
(*she wanted a new bike but she didn't have enough money*)

story problem(s)/literal

_____ 3. What had Mary done to earn money in the past?
(*rake leaves and help around the house*)

problem resolution attempts/literal

_____ 4. Besides Mary, who were the people in the story?
(*Aunt Deb, Mary's family*)

character-characterization/literal

_____ 5. How did Mary finally solve her problem?
(*worked hard for Aunt Deb and earned enough money*)

problem resolution/inferential

_____ 6. What were two things Mary did for Aunt Deb?
(*mopped floor, swept carport, cleaned out flower beds*)

problem resolution attempts/literal

_____ 7. What lesson did Mary learn about getting something you really want?
(*it takes time and hard work*)

theme/evaluative

_____ 8. Why did Mary go to the store the next day?
(*to buy her bike*)

problem resolution attempts/inferential

PART II: ORAL READING AND ANALYSIS OF MISCUES

Directions: Say, "Now I would like to hear you read this story out loud." Have the student read orally until the 100-word sample is completed. Follow along on the Miscue Grid, marking any oral reading errors as appropriate. *Remember to count miscues only up to the point in the story containing the oral reading stop-marker (//).* Then complete the Developmental/Performance Summary to determine whether to continue the assessment. (*Note:* The Miscue Grid should be completed *after* the assessment session has been concluded in order to minimize stress for the student.)

ERROR TYPES   ERROR ANALYSIS

Mary's New Bike	mis-pronun.	sub-stitute	inser-tions	tchr. assist	omis-sions	Error Totals	Self-Correct.	(M) Meaning	(S) Syntax	(V) Visual
Mary wanted a new bike. She helped										
around the house to make money. She had										
even helped her father rake leaves for extra										
money. But she still didn't have the money										
for the new ten-speed bike. One day her										
Aunt Deb came to visit Mary's family.										
Aunt Deb heard that Mary wanted a new										
bike. She told Mary that she had some work										
for her. Mary walked over to Aunt Deb's										
house the very next day. Aunt Deb had Mary										
mop her kitchen floor. Mary cleaned out the										
flower beds. Mary swept out the carport.										
Finally Aunt Deb asked // *Mary to fold*										
her clean clothes.										
TOTALS										

Summary of Reading Behaviors (Strengths and Needs)

PART III: MISCUE ANALYSIS

Directions: *Circle all reading behaviors you observed.*

A. Fundamental Behaviors Observed

L → R Directionality   1 to 1 Matching   Searching for Clues   Cross-Checking

B. Word Attack Behaviors

No Attempt   Mispronunciation (Invented word)   Substitutes

Skips/Reads On   Asks for Help   Repeats   Attempts to Self-Correct

"Sounds Out" (Segmenting)   Blends Sounds   Structural Analysis (Root words, Affixes)

C. Cueing Systems Used in Attempting Words

CUEING TOOL	MISCUE EXAMPLES	ACTUAL TEXT
(M) Meaning		
(S) Syntax		
(V) Visual		

D. Fluency (word by word → fluent reading)

Word by Word _____   Mixed Phrasing _____   Fluent Reading _____   Fluency Rate in Seconds _____

Performance Summary

Silent Reading Comprehension

_____ 0–1 questions missed = Easy

_____ 2 questions missed = Adequate

_____ 3+ questions missed = Too hard

Oral Reading Accuracy

_____ 0–1 oral error = Easy

_____ 2–5 oral errors = Adequate

_____ 6+ oral errors = Too hard

Continue to the next reading passage? _____ Yes   _____ No

PART IV: LISTENING COMPREHENSION

Directions: If you have decided not to continue to have the student read any other passages, then use this passage to begin assessing the student's listening comprehension (see page 19). Begin by reading the background statement for this passage and then say, "I am going to read this story to you. Please listen carefully because I will be asking you some questions after I finish reading it to you." After reading the passage, ask the student the questions associated with the passage. If the student correctly answers more than six questions, you will need to move to the next level and repeat the procedure.

Listening Comprehension

_____ 0–2 questions missed = move to the next passage level

_____ more than 2 questions missed = stop assessment or move down a level

Examiner's Notes

B LEVEL 3 ASSESSMENT PROTOCOLS

Bedtime (246 words)

PART I: SILENT READING COMPREHENSION

Background Statement: "This is a story about a girl who has to go to bed. As you read the story, try to find out why she has to go to bed. Read it carefully because I'm going to ask you to tell me about it."

Teacher Directions: Once the student completes the silent reading, say, "Tell me about the story you just read." Answers to the questions below that the student provides during the retelling should be marked "ua" in the appropriate blank to indicate that this response was unaided. Ask all remaining questions not addressed during the retelling and mark those the student answers with an "a" to indicate that the correct response was given after prompting by the teacher.

Questions/Answers

*Story Grammar Element/
Level of Comprehension*

_____ 1. Who were the people in the story?
(*Wild Willie, Beth, and her mother*)

character-characterization/literal

_____ 2. Where was Wild Willie?
(*the desert*)

setting/inferential

_____ 3. What was Wild Willie's problem?
(*he was being followed*)

story problem(s)/literal

_____ 4. Why didn't Beth find out what was following Wild Willie?
(*TV was turned off*)

story problem(s)/literal

_____ 5. How is Beth going to find out what was following Wild Willie?
(*watch the reruns*)

problem resolution attempts/inferential

_____ 6. If you were Beth, what other way can you think of to find out what was following Wild Willie?
(*ask a friend, or any other plausible response*)

problem resolution/inferential

_____ 7. How would you describe Beth's feelings when she had to go to bed?
(*disappointed, mad, upset, or other plausible responses*)

character-characterization/evaluative

_____ 8. What were the two reasons Beth's mother gave for turning off the TV?
(*it was a school day and it was getting late*)

problem resolution attempts/literal

PART II: ORAL READING AND ANALYSIS OF MISCUES

Directions: Say, "Now I would like to hear you read this story out loud." Have the student read orally until the 100-word sample is completed. Follow along on the Miscue Grid, marking any oral reading errors as appropriate. *Remember to count miscues only up to the point in the story containing the oral reading stop-marker (//).* Then complete the Developmental/Performance Summary to determine whether to continue the assessment. (*Note:* The Miscue Grid should be completed *after* the assessment session has been concluded in order to minimize stress for the student.)

	mis-pronun.	sub-stitute	inser-tions	tchr. assist	omis-sions	Error Totals	Self-Correct.	(M) Meaning	(S) Syntax	(V) Visual
Bedtime										
The sun was going down. The air was										
hot and Wild Willie was afraid. Never										
had he been in such a dry, hot place. His										
horse, Wizard, was trying to find a few										
blades of grass. Wild Willie was beginning										
to fall asleep from staying awake so long.										
Then he heard the sound again—the										
same sound he had been hearing for										
days. What could it be? Why was it										
following him? How could he find out										
what or who it was? Slowly Wizard										
turned around. Willie stood up in the										
stirrups to see over the sand dune. He										
saw // *no one.*										
TOTALS										

Summary of Reading Behaviors (Strengths and Needs)

PART III: MISCUE ANALYSIS

Directions: *Circle all reading behaviors you observed.*

A. Fundamental Behaviors Observed:

L → R Directionality   1 to 1 Matching   Searching for Clues   Cross-Checking

B. Word Attack Behaviors:

No Attempt   Mispronunciation (Invented word)   Substitutes

Skips/Reads On   Asks for Help   Repeats   Attempts to Self-Correct

"Sounds Out" (Segmenting)   Blends Sounds   Structural Analysis (Root words, Affixes)

C. Cueing Systems Used in Attempting Words

CUEING TOOL	MISCUE EXAMPLES	ACTUAL TEXT
(M) Meaning		
(S) Syntax		
(V) Visual		

D. Fluency (word by word → fluent reading)

Word by Word _____   Mixed Phrasing _____   Fluent Reading _____   Fluency Rate in Seconds _____

Performance Summary

Silent Reading Comprehension

_____ 0–1 questions missed = Easy

_____ 2 questions missed = Adequate

_____ 3+ questions missed = Too hard

Oral Reading Accuracy

_____ 0–1 oral error = Easy

_____ 2–5 oral errors = Adequate

_____ 6+ oral errors = Too hard

Continue to the next reading passage? _____ Yes   _____ No

PART IV: LISTENING COMPREHENSION

Directions: If you have decided not to continue to have the student read any other passages, then use this passage to begin assessing the student's listening comprehension (see page 19). Begin by reading the background statement for this passage and then say, "I am going to read this story to you. Please listen carefully because I will be asking you some questions after I finish reading it to you." After reading the passage, ask the student the questions associated with the passage. If the student correctly answers more than six questions, you will need to move to the next level and repeat the procedure.

Listening Comprehension

_____ 0–2 questions missed = move to the next passage level

_____ more than 2 questions missed = stop assessment or move down a level

Examiner's Notes:

LEVEL 4 ASSESSMENT PROTOCOLS

A Different Time (294 words)

PART I: SILENT READING COMPREHENSION

Background Statement: "This story is about a boy who lived a long time ago. Read the story to find out what Marlo wanted and why he couldn't have it. Read it carefully because I will ask you to tell me about it when you finish."

Teacher Directions: Once the student completes the silent reading, say, "Tell me about the story you just read." Answers to the questions below that the student provides during the retelling should be marked "ua" in the appropriate blank to indicate that this response was unaided. Ask all remaining questions not addressed during the retelling and mark those the student answers with an "a" to indicate that the correct response was given after prompting by the teacher.

Questions/Answers

Story Grammar Element/ Level of Comprehension

_____ 1. Where did Marlo live?
  (in a hut)

setting/literal

_____ 2. What was Marlo's problem?
  (he wanted to read)

story problem(s)/literal

_____ 3. What did Marlo do that caused the old man to help him?
  (gave him some vegetables)

problem resolution attempts/inferential

_____ 4. Where did Marlo have to meet the old man?
  (old oak tree)

setting/literal

_____ 5. How was Marlo's problem solved?
  (the old man gave him a book so he could learn to read)

problem resolution attempts/inferential

_____ 6. How would you describe Marlo?
  (kind, nice, thankful, other plausible responses)

character-characterization/evaluative

_____ 7. How do you know that this story took place in olden times and not today?
  (castle, they lived in hut, used a cart, lots of people couldn't read, and other plausible responses)

setting/inferential

_____ 8. Why is "be kind to others and they'll be kind to you" a good theme for this story?
  (responses will vary but should indicate that Marlo got his wish because of his kindness)

theme/evaluative

PART II: ORAL READING AND ANALYSIS OF MISCUES

Directions: Say, "Now I would like to hear you read this story out loud." Have the student read orally until the 100-word sample is completed. Follow along on the Miscue Grid, marking any oral reading errors as appropriate. *Remember to count miscues only up to the point in the story containing the oral reading stop-marker (//)*. Then complete the Developmental/Performance Summary to determine whether to continue the assessment. (*Note:* The Miscue Grid should be completed *after* the assessment session has been concluded in order to minimize stress for the student.)

ERROR TYPES | ERROR ANALYSIS

	mis-pronun.	sub-stitute	inser-tions	tchr. assist	omis-sions	Error Totals	Self-Correct.	(M) Meaning	(S) Syntax	(V) Visual
A Different Time										
Marlo lived in a different time and a										
different place. He lived in a time of										
darkness and gloom. Marlo lived in a										
small hut with his poor parents. He didn't have										
nice clothes and he didn't have much to eat.										
But neither of these things bothered Marlo.										
There was only one thing he wanted. But										
he couldn't have it because the ruler										
would not let any of his people have it.										
This most important thing was to be able										
to read. Today this may seem like a										
dumb wish, but to Marlo it wasn't. One										
day Marlo's father sent // *him*										
to the castle with a cart of vegetables.										
TOTALS										

Summary of Reading Behaviors (Strengths and Needs)

PART III: MISCUE ANALYSIS

Directions: *Circle all reading behaviors you observed.*

A. Fundamental Behaviors Observed:

L → R Directionality   1 to 1 Matching   Searching for Clues   Cross-Checking

B. Word Attack Behaviors:

No Attempt   Mispronunciation (Invented word)   Substitutes

Skips/Reads On   Asks for Help   Repeats   Attempts to Self-Correct

"Sounds Out" (Segmenting)   Blends Sounds   Structural Analysis (Root words, Affixes)

C. Cueing Systems Used in Attempting Words

CUEING TOOL	MISCUE EXAMPLES	ACTUAL TEXT
(M) Meaning		
(S) Syntax		
(V) Visual		

D. Fluency (word by word → fluent reading)

Word by Word _____   Mixed Phrasing _____   Fluent Reading _____   Fluency Rate in Seconds _____

Performance Summary

Silent Reading Comprehension

_____ 0–1 questions missed = Easy

_____ 2 questions missed = Adequate

_____ 3+ questions missed = Too hard

Oral Reading Accuracy

_____ 0–1 oral error = Easy

_____ 2–5 oral errors = Adequate

_____ 6+ oral errors = Too hard

Continue to the next reading passage? _____ Yes   _____ No

PART IV: LISTENING COMPREHENSION

Directions: If you have decided not to continue to have the student read any other passages, then use this passage to begin assessing the student's listening comprehension (see page 19). Begin by reading the background statement for this passage and then say, "I am going to read this story to you. Please listen carefully because I will be asking you some questions after I finish reading it to you." After reading the passage, ask the student the questions associated with the passage. If the student correctly answers more than six questions, you will need to move to the next level and repeat the procedure.

Listening Comprehension

_____ 0–2 questions missed = move to the next passage level

_____ more than 2 questions missed = stop assessment or move down a level

Examiner's Notes

PART I: SILENT READING COMPREHENSION

Background Statement: "This story is about a young girl who goes walking in woods that are supposed to be haunted. Read the story to find out what happens to Allison when she ventures into the haunted woods. Read it carefully because I will ask you to tell me about it when you finish."

Teacher Directions: Once the student completes the silent reading, say, "Tell me about the story you just read." Answers to the questions below that the student provides during the retelling should be marked "ua" in the appropriate blank to indicate that this response was unaided. Ask all remaining questions not addressed during the retelling and mark those the student answers with an "a" to indicate that the correct response was given after prompting by the teacher.

Questions/Answers	*Story Grammar Element/ Level of Comprehension*
_____ 1. Who is the main character in this story? *(Allison)*	character-characterization/literal
_____ 2. Where was Allison when she first met the old lady? *(in the woods or under an elm tree)*	setting/literal
_____ 3. Where did the old woman take Allison? *(to the old woman's hut)*	setting/literal
_____ 4. What was Allison's problem with the old woman? *(getting away before being sold to the dwarf or not acting tired)*	story problem(s)/inferential
_____ 5. How did Allison escape from the old woman? *(she ran out the door while the woman was looking for her dog)*	problem resolution/literal
_____ 6. What happened after Allison couldn't run any farther and fell asleep? *(her brother woke her up)*	problem resolution attempts/literal
_____ 7. What happened after Allison was safely back home? *(she found a small metal tag with "Spirit" printed on it)*	problem resolution attempts/literal
_____ 8. Why, in the story, did Allison always tell the old woman that she was not tired? *(because she didn't want to be sold)*	problem resolution attempts/inferential

PART II: ORAL READING AND ANALYSIS OF MISCUES

Directions: Say, "Now I would like to hear you read this story out loud." Have the student read orally until the 100-word sample is completed. Follow along on the Miscue Grid, marking any oral reading errors as appropriate. *Remember to count miscues only up to the point in the story containing the oral reading stop-marker (//).* Then complete the Developmental/Performance Summary to determine whether to continue the assessment. (*Note:* The Miscue Grid should be completed *after* the assessment session has been concluded in order to minimize stress for the student.)

ERROR TYPES

ERROR ANALYSIS

Afternoon Walk	mis-pronun.	sub-stitute	inser-tions	tchr. assist	omis-sions	Error Totals	Self-Correct.	(M) Meaning	(S) Syntax	(V) Visual
One day Allison was walking in the										
woods behind her house. Some of the										
other children in the neighborhood liked										
to tease her by saying that the woods were										
haunted. "There's an old, withered,										
witch-like woman in those woods who										
comes out at two o'clock every day to										
catch children," they'd say. "She makes										
them do housework and things like that.										
Then she sells them to a grim looking										
dwarf from far away when they are										
too tired to work. Once captured they										
are never seen again." Allison knew her										
friends were only telling stories,										
but it still frightened // her sometimes										
when she went into the woods.										
TOTALS										

Summary of Reading Behaviors (Strengths and Needs)

PART III: MISCUE ANALYSIS

Directions: *Circle all reading behaviors you observed.*

A. Fundamental Behaviors Observed:

L → R Directionality   1 to 1 Matching   Searching for Clues   Cross-Checking

B. Word Attack Behaviors:

No Attempt   Mispronunciation (Invented word)   Substitutes

Skips/Reads On   Asks for Help   Repeats   Attempts to Self-Correct

"Sounds Out" (Segmenting)   Blends Sounds   Structural Analysis (Root words, Affixes)

C. Cueing Systems Used in Attempting Words

CUEING TOOL	MISCUE EXAMPLES	ACTUAL TEXT
(M) Meaning		
(S) Syntax		
(V) Visual		

D. Fluency (word by word → fluent reading)

Word by Word _____   Mixed Phrasing _____   Fluent Reading _____   Fluency Rate in Seconds _____

Performance Summary

Silent Reading Comprehension

_____ 0–1 questions missed = Easy

_____ 2 questions missed = Adequate

_____ 3+ questions missed = Too hard

Oral Reading Accuracy

_____ 0–1 oral error = Easy

_____ 2–5 oral errors = Adequate

_____ 6+ oral errors = Too hard

Continue to the next reading passage? _____ Yes   _____ No

PART IV: LISTENING COMPREHENSION

Directions: If you have decided not to continue to have the student read any other passages, then use this passage to begin assessing the student's listening comprehension (see page 19). Begin by reading the background statement for this passage and then say, "I am going to read this story to you. Please listen carefully because I will be asking you some questions after I finish reading it to you." After reading the passage, ask the student the questions associated with the passage. If the student correctly answers more than six questions, you will need to move to the next level and repeat the procedure.

Listening Comprehension

_____ 0–2 questions missed = move to the next passage level

_____ more than 2 questions missed = stop assessment or move down a level

Examiner's Notes:

LEVEL 6 ASSESSMENT PROTOCOLS

Laser Boy (379 words)

PART I: SILENT READING COMPREHENSION

Background Statement: "This story is about a boy who had problems in school. Read the story to find out how the boy's problems were solved. Read it carefully because I'm going to ask you to tell me about it when you finish."

Teacher Directions: Once the student completes the silent reading, say, "Tell me about the story you just read." Answers to the questions below that the student provides during the retelling should be marked "ua" in the appropriate blank to indicate that this response was unaided. Ask all remaining questions not addressed during the retelling and mark those the student answers with an "a" to indicate that the correct response was given after prompting by the teacher.

Questions/Answers	*Story Grammar Element/ Level of Comprehension*
_____ 1. Who was the story mainly about? *(Matthew)*	character-characterization/literal
_____ 2. What was Matthew's problem? *(he wasn't doing well in school, or other plausible responses)*	story problem(s)/inferential
_____ 3. What did Matthew's teacher decide to do about Matthew's problem? *(have Matthew tested for a learning problem)*	problem resolution attempts/literal
_____ 4. Summarize what the school found out about Matthew's problem. *(he was gifted in math and science)*	problem resolution/inferential
_____ 5. How did the school try to solve the problem? *(it allowed Matthew to study what interested him the most)*	problem resolution attempts/inferential
_____ 6. How was Matthew affected by being allowed to study what most interested him? *(he improved as a student and made friends)*	character-characterization/inferential
_____ 7. How did Matthew's story affect the writer of this story? *(the writer believes everyone has special talents if you look for them)*	theme/evaluative
_____ 8. Why were the phone calls with the professor set up for Matthew? *(so he could ask the professor about lasers when he needed to)*	problem resolution attempts/literal

PART II: ORAL READING AND ANALYSIS OF MISCUES

Directions: Say, "Now I would like to hear you read this story out loud." Have the student read orally until the 100-word sample is completed. Follow along on the Miscue Grid, marking any oral reading errors as appropriate. *Remember to count miscues only up to the point in the story containing the oral reading stop-marker (//).* Then complete the Developmental/Performance Summary to determine whether to continue the assessment. (*Note:* The Miscue Grid should be completed *after* the assessment session has been concluded in order to minimize stress for the student.)

ERROR TYPES   ERROR ANALYSIS

Laser Boy	mis-pronun.	sub-stitute	inser-tions	tchr. assist	omis-sions	Error Totals	Self-Correct.	(M) Meaning	(S) Syntax	(V) Visual
My name is Bob and I'm a teacher.										
Several years ago I knew a student										
that I'd like to tell you about.										
Matthew was a 13-year-old who never										
seemed to do well in school. Some										
say that he was a misfit, someone										
who doesn't quite fit in with the										
other kids his age. Not only that,										
Matthew had trouble in school nearly										
his whole life. He failed to complete his										
homework even when it was an easy assignment.										
By not participating in class, not turning in										
homework, and only doing a fair job on tests,										
Matthew always seemed to // *be just barely passing.*										
TOTALS										

Summary of Reading Behaviors (Strengths and Needs)

PART III: MISCUE ANALYSIS

Directions: *Circle all reading behaviors you observed.*

A. Fundamental Behaviors Observed:

L → R Directionality   1 to 1 Matching   Searching for Clues   Cross-Checking

B. Word Attack Behaviors

No Attempt   Mispronunciation (Invented word)   Substitutes

Skips/Reads On   Asks for Help   Repeats   Attempts to Self-Correct

"Sounds Out" (Segmenting)   Blends Sounds   Structural Analysis (Root words, Affixes)

C. Cueing Systems Used in Attempting Words

CUEING TOOL	MISCUE EXAMPLES	ACTUAL TEXT
(M) Meaning		
(S) Syntax		
(V) Visual		

D. Fluency (word by word → fluent reading)

Word by Word _____   Mixed Phrasing _____   Fluent Reading _____   Fluency Rate in Seconds _____

Performance Summary

Silent Reading Comprehension

_____ 0–1 questions missed = Easy

_____ 2 questions missed = Adequate

_____ 3+ questions missed = Too hard

Oral Reading Accuracy

_____ 0–1 oral error = Easy

_____ 2–5 oral errors = Adequate

_____ 6+ oral errors = Too hard

Continue to the next reading passage? _____ Yes   _____ No

PART IV: LISTENING COMPREHENSION

Directions: If you have decided not to continue to have the student read any other passages, then use this passage to begin assessing the student's listening comprehension (see page 19). Begin by reading the background statement for this passage and then say, "I am going to read this story to you. Please listen carefully because I will be asking you some questions after I finish reading it to you." After reading the passage, ask the student the questions associated with the passage. If the student correctly answers more than six questions, you will need to move to the next level and repeat the procedure.

Listening Comprehension

_____ 0–2 questions missed = move to the next passage level

_____ more than 2 questions missed = stop assessment or move down a level

Examiner's Notes

LEVEL 7 ASSESSMENT PROTOCOLS

The Paper Route (435 words)

PART I: SILENT READING COMPREHENSION

Background Statement: "This story is about a boy who begins his first job as a paperboy. Read it to find out what his first year as a paperboy was like. Read it carefully because I will ask you to tell me about it when you finish."

Teacher Directions: Once the student completes the silent reading, say, "Tell me about the story you just read." Answers to the questions below that the student provides during the retelling should be marked "ua" in the appropriate blank to indicate that this response was unaided. Ask all remaining questions not addressed during the retelling and mark those the student answers with an "a" to indicate that the correct response was given after prompting by the teacher.

Questions/Answers	*Story Grammar Element/ Level of Comprehension*
_____ 1. Who were the main characters in the story? *(Scott and Mr. Miley)*	character-characterization/literal
_____ 2. How did Scott get a chance to earn money? *(by answering an ad for newspaper carriers)*	problem resolution attempts/literal
_____ 3. What did Scott have to do each morning after picking up his newspapers? *(roll them and put them in plastic bags)*	problem resolution attempts/literal
_____ 4. Why were Thursdays and Sundays problems for Scott? *(papers were extra large and it took many trips to get them delivered)*	story problem(s)/inferential
_____ 5. What were the two main problems Scott faced with his job? *(bad weather and cranky customers)*	story problem(s)/literal
_____ 6. How did Scott handle the problem of cranky customers? *(by going out of his way to please them)*	problem resolution/literal
_____ 7. What words would you use to describe Scott? *(responses will vary but should reflect the idea of hardworking, conscientious)*	character-characterization/evaluative
_____ 8. What lessons would a job like Scott's teach? *(responses will vary but should indicate a theme related to benefits of hard work)*	theme/evaluative

PART II: ORAL READING AND ANALYSIS OF MISCUES

Directions: Say, "Now I would like to hear you read this story out loud." Have the student read orally until the 100-word sample is completed. Follow along on the Miscue Grid, marking any oral reading errors as appropriate. *Remember to count miscues only up to the point in the story containing the oral reading stop-marker (//).* Then complete the Developmental/Performance Summary to determine whether to continue the assessment. (*Note:* The Miscue Grid should be completed *after* the assessment session has been concluded in order to minimize stress for the student.)

ERROR TYPES   **ERROR ANALYSIS**

The Paper Route	mis-pronun.	sub-stitute	inser-tions	tchr. assist	omis-sions	Error Totals	Self-Correct.	(M) Meaning	(S) Syntax	(V) Visual
Scott had a chance to earn his own money										
for the first time. Answering an advertisement										
for newspaper carriers, he set up an appointment										
with Mr. Miley, the distribution manager.										
Mr. Miley was a rather short and stocky										
man who spoke with a loud voice. After										
reviewing Scott's application, Mr. Miley										
said, "You look like a dependable young										
man to me. Do your parents approve of										
your becoming a paperboy?" "Yes, sir,"										
replied Scott, "and I have a letter from my										
Dad saying it's OK with him." "You										
can have the job, Scott," said Mr. Miley.										
"However, I want you // to realize that this is										
a long route and you will have to get up very early.										
TOTALS										

Summary of Reading Behaviors (Strengths and Needs)

PART III: MISCUE ANALYSIS

Directions: Circle all reading behaviors you observed.

A. Fundamental Behaviors Observed

L → R Directionality   1 to 1 Matching   Searching for Clues   Cross-Checking

B. Word Attack Behaviors

No Attempt   Mispronunciation (Invented word)   Substitutes

Skips/Reads On   Asks for Help   Repeats   Attempts to Self-Correct

"Sounds Out" (Segmenting)   Blends Sounds   Structural Analysis (Root words, Affixes)

C. Cueing Systems Used in Attempting Words

CUEING TOOL	MISCUE EXAMPLES	ACTUAL TEXT
(M) Meaning		
(S) Syntax		
(V) Visual		

D. Fluency (word by word → fluent reading)

Word by Word _____   Mixed Phrasing _____   Fluent Reading _____   Fluency Rate in Seconds _____

Performance Summary

Silent Reading Comprehension

_____ 0–1 questions missed = Easy

_____ 2 questions missed = Adequate

_____ 3+ questions missed = Too hard

Oral Reading Accuracy

_____ 0–1 oral error = Easy

_____ 2–5 oral errors = Adequate

_____ 6+ oral errors = Too hard

Continue to the next reading passage? _____ Yes   _____ No

PART IV: LISTENING COMPREHENSION

Directions: If you have decided not to continue to have the student read any other passages, then use this passage to begin assessing the student's listening comprehension (see page 19). Begin by reading the background statement for this passage and then say, "I am going to read this story to you. Please listen carefully because I will be asking you some questions after I finish reading it to you." After reading the passage, ask the student the questions associated with the passage. If the student correctly answers more than six questions, you will need to move to the next level and repeat the procedure.

Listening Comprehension

_____ 0–2 questions missed = move to the next passage level

_____ more than 2 questions missed = stop assessment or move down a level

Examiner's Notes:

LEVEL 8 ASSESSMENT PROTOCOLS

Riley and Leonard (430 words)

PART I: SILENT READING COMPREHENSION

Background Statement: "This is a story about a boy named Leonard who was very unpopular in school. Read this story to find out how Leonard deals with his problem. Read it carefully because I'm going to ask you to tell me about it when you finish."

Teacher Directions: Once the student completes the silent reading, say, "Tell me about the story you just read." Answers to the questions below that the student provides during the retelling should be marked "ua" in the appropriate blank to indicate that this response was unaided. Ask all remaining questions not addressed during the retelling and mark those the student answers with an "a" to indicate that the correct response was given after prompting by the teacher.

Questions/Answers

Story Grammar Element/ Level of Comprehension

_____ 1. Who were the main characters in the story?
   (Leonard, Riley, Lorrie)

character-characterization/literal

_____ 2. What was Leonard's problem when he was in school?
   (he was unpopular)

story problem(s)/literal

_____ 3. What problem resolution attempts did Leonard make when his fellow students made negative comments about his family?
   (he started a fight)

problem resolution attempts/literal

_____ 4. How did the fight end?
   (Leonard was forced to give up; he lost)

problem resolution attempts/literal

_____ 5. How did Leonard solve his problem of being unpopular?
   (by becoming successful and involved in civic projects)

problem resolution/inferential

_____ 6. Where did the accident take place?
   (outside the fancy restaurant)

setting/literal

_____ 7. What caused the beggar to step into the path of the truck?
   (surprise at both the amount of money and the fact that it was Leonard)

problem resolution attempts/inferential

_____ 8. What is the theme/moral of this passage?
   (responses will vary but should indicate a theme/ moral related to "what goes around comes around")

theme/evaluative

PART II: ORAL READING AND ANALYSIS OF MISCUES

Directions: Say, "Now I would like to hear you read this story out loud." Have the student read orally until the 100-word sample is completed. Follow along on the Miscue Grid, marking any oral reading errors as appropriate. *Remember to count miscues only up to the point in the story containing the oral reading stop-marker (//).* Then complete the Developmental/Performance Summary to determine whether to continue the assessment. (*Note:* The Miscue Grid should be completed *after* the assessment session has been concluded in order to minimize stress for the student.)

ERROR TYPES

ERROR ANALYSIS

Riley and Leonard

	mis-pronun.	sub-stitute	inser-tions	tchr. assist	omis-sions	Error Totals	Self-Correct.	(M) Meaning	(S) Syntax	(V) Visual
At times Leonard felt like the most										
unpopular boy in school. No matter what										
he did he was constantly ridiculed by his classmates.										
Maybe it was because he was small in stature										
and wore thick bifocals. Or maybe it was										
because he didn't like sports. Possibly										
it was because he couldn't afford the designer										
clothes the other kids seemed to live for.										
Regardless, Leonard felt like a loser and										
was unhappy with his situation. One										
day, while putting his books in his locker,										
the familiar mockery began. A small covey										
of classmates formed a semicircle around										
Leonard. Each began to // taunt him										
and call him names.										
TOTALS										

Summary of Reading Behaviors (Strengths and Needs)

PART III: MISCUE ANALYSIS

Directions: *Circle all reading behaviors you observed.*

A. Fundamental Behaviors Observed:

L → R Directionality   1 to 1 Matching   Searching for Clues   Cross-Checking

B. Word Attack Behaviors:

No Attempt   Mispronunciation (Invented word)   Substitutes

Skips/Reads On   Asks for Help   Repeats   Attempts to Self-Correct

"Sounds Out" (Segmenting)   Blends Sounds   Structural Analysis (Root words, Affixes)

C. Cueing Systems Used in Attempting Words

CUEING TOOL	MISCUE EXAMPLES	ACTUAL TEXT
(M) Meaning		
(S) Syntax		
(V) Visual		

D. Fluency (word by word → fluent reading)

Word by Word _____   Mixed Phrasing _____   Fluent Reading _____   Fluency Rate in Seconds _____

Performance Summary

Silent Reading Comprehension

_____ 0–1 questions missed = Easy

_____ 2 questions missed = Adequate

_____ 3+ questions missed = Too hard

Oral Reading Accuracy

_____ 0–1 oral error = Easy

_____ 2–5 oral errors = Adequate

_____ 6+ oral errors = Too hard

Continue to the next reading passage? _____ Yes   _____ No

PART IV: LISTENING COMPREHENSION

Directions: If you have decided not to continue to have the student read any other passages, then use this passage to begin assessing the student's listening comprehension (see page 19). Begin by reading the background statement for this passage and then say, "I am going to read this story to you. Please listen carefully because I will be asking you some questions after I finish reading it to you." After reading the passage, ask the student the questions associated with the passage. If the student correctly answers more than six questions, you will need to move to the next level and repeat the procedure.

Listening Comprehension

_____ 0–2 questions missed = move to the next passage level

_____ more than 2 questions missed = stop assessment or move down a level

Examiner's Notes:

LEVEL 9 ASSESSMENT PROTOCOLS

The Long Night (474 words)

PART I: SILENT READING COMPREHENSION

Background Statement: "This story is about mistaken identity. Read it carefully because I will ask you to tell me about the story when you finish reading."

Teacher Directions: Once the student completes the silent reading, say, "Tell me about the story you just read." Answers to the questions below that the student provides during the retelling should be marked "ua" in the appropriate blank to indicate that this response was unaided. Ask all remaining questions not addressed during the retelling and mark those the student answers with an "a" to indicate that the correct response was given after prompting by the teacher.

Questions/Answers

Story Grammar Element/ Level of Comprehension

_____ 1. Where and at what time of day did this story take place?
(*nighttime in New Orleans*)

setting/literal

_____ 2. What was the problem facing the writer of this story while he walked up Rampart?
(*he was being followed and someone gave him a note that said he was going to die*)

story problem(s)/inferential

_____ 3. How did the policeman react to his story?
(*didn't really believe him*)

problem resolution attempts/literal

_____ 4. What happened after he left the policeman?
(*he was taken into a building by two men*)

problem resolution attempts/literal

_____ 5. How did the writer of this story solve the problem(s)?
(*it turned out to be a case of mistaken identity*)

problem resolution/inferential

_____ 6. Who was Nero, and how would you describe him?
(*he was the boss, a criminal, and a nasty kind of character*)

story problem(s)/inferential

_____ 7. What series of events got the person in this story into such trouble?
(*flight delay, walking alone at night, and he looked like someone else*)

story problem(s)/inferential

_____ 8. What did the author do after he was released?
(*stayed two more days and never returned*)

problem resolution attempts/literal

PART II: ORAL READING AND ANALYSIS OF MISCUES

Directions: Say, "Now I would like to hear you read this story out loud." Have the student read orally until the 100-word sample is completed. Follow along on the Miscue Grid, marking any oral reading errors as appropriate. *Remember to count miscues only up to the point in the story containing the oral reading stop-marker (//).* Then complete the Developmental/Performance Summary to determine whether to continue the assessment. (*Note:* The Miscue Grid should be completed *after* the assessment session has been concluded in order to minimize stress for the student.)

ERROR TYPES

ERROR ANALYSIS

	mis-pronun.	sub-stitute	inser-tions	tchr. assist	omis-sions	Error Totals	Self-Correct.	(M) Meaning	(S) Syntax	(V) Visual
The Long Night										
I arrived late at the New Orleans International										
Airport because of delays in St. Louis. The										
night was descending on the Crescent City as										
I entered the cab for the short ride to city										
center. As the cab headed toward the city,										
the cabbie engaged me in an informative										
conversation about the Crescent City.										
She had an island accent and her multicolored										
dress was very nontraditional. After I told										
her I wanted to go to Rampart in the										
French Quarter, she abruptly turned										
left and headed southwest. Fifteen minutes										
later, without a word, I got out of the										
cab and // *proceeded up Rampart.*										
TOTALS										

Summary of Reading Behaviors (Strengths and Needs)

PART III: MISCUE ANALYSIS

Directions: *Circle all reading behaviors you observed.*

A. Fundamental Behaviors Observed:

L → R Directionality   1 to 1 Matching   Searching for Clues   Cross-Checking

B. Word Attack Behaviors:

No Attempt   Mispronunciation (Invented word)   Substitutes

Skips/Reads On   Asks for Help Repeats   Attempts to Self-Correct

"Sounds Out" (Segmenting)   Blends Sounds   Structural Analysis (Root words, Affixes)

C. Cueing Systems Used in Attempting Words

CUEING TOOL	MISCUE EXAMPLES	ACTUAL TEXT
(M) Meaning		
(S) Syntax		
(V) Visual		

D. Fluency (word by word → fluent reading)

Word by Word _____   Mixed Phrasing _____   Fluent Reading _____   Fluency Rate in Seconds _____

Performance Summary

Silent Reading Comprehension

_____ 0–1 questions missed = Easy

_____ 2 questions missed = Adequate

_____ 3+ questions missed = Too hard

Oral Reading Accuracy

_____ 0–1 oral error = Easy

_____ 2–5 oral errors = Adequate

_____ 6+ oral errors = Too hard

Continue to the next reading passage? _____ Yes   _____ No

PART IV: LISTENING COMPREHENSION

Directions: If you have decided not to continue to have the student read any other passages, then use this passage to begin assessing the student's listening comprehension (see page 19). Begin by reading the background statement for this passage and then say, "I am going to read this story to you. Please listen carefully because I will be asking you some questions after I finish reading it to you." After reading the passage, ask the student the questions associated with the passage. If the student correctly answers more than six questions, you will need to move to the next level and repeat the procedure.

Listening Comprehension

_____ 0–2 questions missed = move to the next passage level

_____ more than 2 questions missed = stop assessment or move down a level

Examiner's Notes:

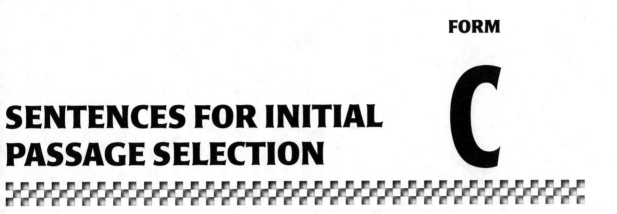

SENTENCES FOR INITIAL PASSAGE SELECTION

FORM C: LEVEL 1

1. Some animals are fun.

2. I eat lots of food.

3. He can smell good.

FORM C: LEVEL 2

1. It was a very clear night.

2. I get hot when the sun shines bright.

3. We can't see air moving.

FORM C: LEVEL 3

1. Many insects are very helpful.

2. Some adults are slender, some are fat.

3. I agree that it is the most beautiful flower.

FORM C: LEVEL 4

1. A famous man would know what to do.

2. The invention was very important.

3. Instead of jam I like syrup on my food.

FORM C: LEVEL 5

1. The estimate for my car was not acceptable.

2. Various people came immediately to the fire.

3. The amount of water you drink is important.

FORM C: LEVEL 6

1. He considered it carefully, but it was too expensive.

2. The new method of raising the temperature got good results.

3. What is common today is the result of many years of experimenting.

FORM C: LEVEL 7

1. Scientists hope to transform the industrial site before the end of the year.

2. Foreign minerals are used to develop usable compounds.

3. The presence of impurities lowers the value of all gems.

FORM C: LEVEL 8

1. Scientists are always looking for advancements to improve the world.

2. The prearranged site was eliminated.

3. To compress hundreds of wires into one is called "fiber optics."

FORM C: LEVEL 9

1. He moved in a circular motion, then ran off laterally.

2. The vertical object couldn't be viewed easily.

3. At the intersection, a series of accidents occurred.

EXPOSITORY PASSAGES

Bears

There are many kinds of bears.
Some bears are brown. Others are black.
Still others are white and are called polar bears.
The biggest bears are called grizzly bears.

Bears can smell and hear very well.
Bears have small eyes and cannot see very well.
They eat all kinds of food.
They eat small animals, plants, and berries.
Most bears sleep during the winter.
When they wake up they are hungry.

Bears can run very fast.
They can climb trees.
They are not safe animals to be around.
The best place to be around bears is at the zoo.

The Night Sky

Look up at the sky at night. If it is a clear night, you will see stars. How many stars are there? No one knows for sure. But there is one star that you know by name. You can see it in the daytime. It is our sun. The sun is a star. All stars are suns. Our sun is so close that we cannot see other stars in the day. We only see the other suns at night.

Stars are made up of very hot gas, and they seem to twinkle because of the air moving across them. Even though we can't always see them, they are always in the sky, even in the daytime.

Flying Flowers

There are many kinds of insects. There are big ones, little ones, ugly ones, biting ones, and helpful ones. But there is one kind of insect that most people agree is the most beautiful one. This insect is often called the flying flower. It is the butterfly.

Butterflies are insects that have two pairs of wings. The wings are covered with tiny scales. The scales are different colors. These scales give the butterfly its beautiful colors. Butterflies smell and hear by using their long, thin antennae. Butterflies can't bite or chew. They use long, tube-like tongues to get at the food they eat from flowers.

Butterflies begin as eggs. Then they hatch into caterpillars. A caterpillar forms a hard skin. When they finally break out of the hard skin, they are butterflies with colorful wings. Adult butterflies must lay eggs soon. They do not live very long.

Butterflies and moths are different. Butterflies like the day. Moths like the night. Moths are not as colorful as butterflies. Butterfly bodies are slender, while moths tend to have large, fat bodies. Moths form cocoons before turning into winged insects. Most butterflies do not form cocoons.

The Story of Coca-Cola

Lots of people all over the world have heard of the soft drink
called Coca-Cola. But not many people know the real story about
how this drink was invented.

Coca-Cola was the invention of a Mr. John Pemberton. Although
he wasn't a doctor, most people called him Dr. Pemberton. He was a
druggist in a town in the South. Dr. Pemberton liked to invent new
things. He lived during the time just after the Civil War.

One day Dr. Pemberton decided to make a headache medicine. He
made it from nuts, fruits, and leaves. He also added the drugs
necessary to cure a headache. Dr. Pemberton now thought he had
something to sell that tasted good.

In the summer of 1886, Dr. Pemberton took a jug of this headache
syrup to one of the best drugstores in Atlanta, Georgia. He told the
manager of the drugstore to mix some of the syrup with water and
have just people with headaches drink it. At first it did not sell very
well. Then one day a clerk sold some of the new medicine to a
customer with a bad headache. But instead of using regular water, he
used carbonated water by accident. Carbonated water has bubbles in
it. Everyone loved this new change, and carbonated water is still used
in Coca-Cola today.

Most of the medicine that cures headaches was taken out of Coca-Cola as time went on. But Dr. Pemberton's drink is still one of the world's favorite soft drinks.

Popcorn

There are three major types of corn grown in this country. First, there is the type of corn people eat most of the time. It is called sweet corn because of its flavor. Second, there is field corn, which is used mainly for feeding livestock. Sometimes people eat field corn too. However, its taste is not as good as sweet corn and its kernels are not as full. The third type of corn, often called Indian corn, is popcorn. Popcorn is grown commercially in the United States because the average American eats almost two pounds of popcorn a year, according to various estimates.

When America was discovered by Columbus, Native Americans had been eating popcorn for thousands of years. They prepared it several different ways. One way was to stick the ear of corn on a stick and place it over a campfire. Any kernels that popped out of the fire were gathered up and eaten. Another method was to scrape the cob and throw the kernels into the fire. Any kernels that popped out of the fire were immediately eaten. Since these methods limited how many kernels could actually be eaten, the Native Americans began to use small clay bowls that they would heat sand in. When the sand got really hot, they placed the popcorn in the bowls and waited for the kernels to pop.

Popcorn is popcorn because of the amount of water content of the kernel. Most experts agree that, ideally, a kernel should have at least fourteen percent water content to be good corn for popping. If the corn kernels have less than twelve percent water content, then the kernels will be duds. They won't pop right.

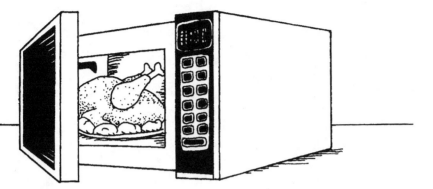

Cooking Without Fire: The Microwave Oven

Microwave cooking is very common today. It is, however, a recent invention. The microwave oven one uses today was developed from the invention of the magnetron tube in 1940. The invention of the magnetron tube, by Sir John Randall and Dr. H. A. Boot, was a very important part of the radar defense of England during World War II. Neither man considered it as a means of preparing food after they invented it.

It wasn't until the late 1940s that Dr. Percy Spencer discovered the magnetron's ability to heat and cook food from the inside out. Spencer experimented with many different foods, all with the same results: The inside got hot first.

It took several years for the company Spencer worked for to develop what we know today as the microwave oven. Not until around 1952 could a person purchase a microwave oven, then called a Radar Range, for home use. These early models were expensive and bulky.

Today's microwave ovens are inexpensive and come with a variety of features. The features include: defrost, constant temperature cooking, and automatic reheat. Microwave cooking, many claim, was the first completely new method of cooking food since early humans discovered fire. Why? Because microwave cooking requires no fire or element of fire to cook food. The food is cooked by electronmagnetic energy.

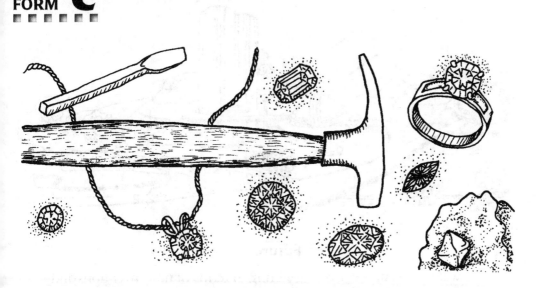

Diamonds

A diamond is one of the most beautiful treasures that nature ever created, and one of the rarest. It takes thousands of years for nature to transform a chunk of carbon into a rough diamond. Only three important diamond fields have been found in the world—in India, South America, and Africa.

The first diamonds were found in the sand and gravel of stream beds. These types of diamonds are called alluvial diamonds. Later, diamonds were found deep in the earth in rock formations called pipes. These formations resemble extinct volcanoes. The rock in which diamonds are found is called blue ground. Yet even where diamonds are plentiful, it takes digging and sorting through tons of rock and gravel to find enough diamonds for a one-carat ring.

Gem diamonds' quality is based on weight, purity, color, and cut. The weight of a diamond is measured by the carat. Its purity is determined by the presence or absence of impurities, such as foreign minerals and uncrystallized carbon. The color of diamonds varies, but most diamonds are tinged yellow or brown. The cut of a diamond also figures into its value. A fully cut diamond, often called flawless, would have fifty-eight facets. Facets, or sides, cause the brilliance that is produced when a diamond is struck by light.

Humans have learned how to make artificial diamonds. Manufactured diamonds are placed in a machine that creates the same pressure that exists about two hundred and fifty miles beneath the surface of the earth. Besides intense pressure, the carbon compounds are heated to temperatures over five thousand degrees Fahrenheit. Unfortunately, the created diamonds are small and are used mainly in industrial settings. They have no value as gems.

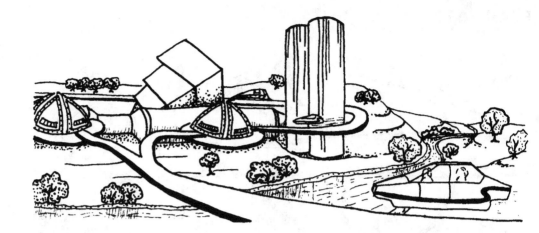

The Future Is Here

What will the twenty-first century bring in terms of new inventions and space-age technologies? No one knows for sure. But scientists, inventors, and futurists are predicting a variety of new inventions. These new advancements will affect the way we live and play. Some of them are already on the drawing board.

One example is the levitation vehicle. The idea of a vertical take-off and landing aircraft that can also be driven on the road is the invention of Paul Moeller. He named his first version of this type of craft the Moeller 400. People involved in this type of technology see increases in population and crowded highways as reasons that a levitation vehicle will be needed. Imagine flying into the city, hovering over a prearranged landing site, landing, and then driving the rest of the way to work.

Another innovation developed in the 1990s is the dental laser. Researchers created a laser that they hope will replace the much feared dental drill. The laser basically vaporizes the cavity without affecting the surrounding enamel. As a bonus, the laser will eliminate the need for a shot to deaden surrounding tissue.

Probably one of the most significant new technologies that will continue to affect people in the future is fiber optics. Fiber optics has the effect of compressing hundreds of wires into one, thus allowing for the communication of huge amounts of information over very thin wires. One example of the application of fiber optics will be the development of full-motion, color video telephones. These will be particularly important to the deaf.

Another advancement that is becoming commonplace in the early twenty-first century is high-definition television. The average consumer will be able to upgrade his or her current televiewing dramatically when high-definition television becomes widely available at affordable prices. The color of these televisions has the vividness of 35-millimeter movies and the sound quality of compact discs (CDs). This refinement will lead to improvements in at-home movies and video games, both of which will be available in three-dimensional formats.

Regardless of new advancements in technology, people must be prepared to face the challenges of the future: namely, to assist each other as we travel through time, and to help preserve our home, the earth.

Visual Illusions

A visual illusion is an unreal or misleading appearance or image, according to *Webster's* dictionary. In other words, visual illusions are sometimes caused by ideas one holds about what one expects to see. In other instances, the illusion is caused by the brain's difficulty in choosing from two or more visual patterns.

If you look at a bull's-eye and move it slowly in circular motions, you should see spokes moving. The spokes, if you see them, aren't really there. This type of visual illusion is called lateral inhibition.

Another type of visual illusion occurs when a person tries to estimate the height of a vertical object. It is referred to as length distortion. The famous Gateway Arch in St. Louis is an example of length distortion, because the arch seems much higher than it is wide. In reality the height and width of the arch are identical. Length distortion occurs because our eyes move more easily from side to side than up and down. This greater effort to look up causes the brain to over-interpret the height of vertical objects.

If you look at a series of squares, you should see small gray spots at each intersection. If you look directly at one intersection, the spots should disappear. This illusion is known as Hermann's Grid. It is often seen in modern high-rise office buildings. Many of these buildings have windows separated by crossing strips of metal or concrete.

The above are only three examples of the many ways that our eyes can deceive us. But they do reinforce the old axiom, "Don't believe everything you see."

EXAMINER'S
ASSESSMENT PROTOCOLS

LEVEL 1 ASSESSMENT PROTOCOLS

Bears (99 words)

PART I: SILENT READING COMPREHENSION

Background Statement: "This story is about bears. Read this story to find out information about the different kinds of bears. Read it carefully because I'm going to ask you to tell me about what you read."

Teacher Directions: Once the student completes the silent reading, say, "Tell me about the story you just read." Answers to the questions below that the student provides during the retelling should be marked "ua" in the appropriate blank to indicate that this response was unaided. Ask all remaining questions not addressed during the retelling and mark those the student answers with an "a" to indicate that the correct response was given after prompting by the teacher.

Questions/Answers *Element*	*Level of Comprehension/* *Expository Grammar*
_____ 1. What kinds of bears did you read about? (*brown, black, polar, and grizzly*)	literal/collection
_____ 2. What kind of bear is the biggest of all? (*grizzly bear*)	literal/description
_____ 3. Explain why bears are not safe to be around. (*accept plausible responses related to bears being wild and having been known to attack humans.*)	inferential/problem-solution
_____ 4. What are some things bears can do very well? (*smell, hear, run, climb—any three*)	literal/collection
_____ 5. How do bears find their food? (*smelling and hearing*)	inferential/problem-solution
_____ 6. Why are bears often hungry after winter? (*because they sleep most of the winter*)	inferential/causation
_____ 7. Can you name two things that bears eat? (*plants, berries, and small animals*)	literal/collection
_____ 8. Where did the story say was the best place to be around bears? (*at the zoo*)	literal/description

PART II: ORAL READING AND ANALYSIS OF MISCUES

Directions: Say, "Now I would like to hear you read this story out loud." Have the student read orally until the sample is completed. Follow along on the Miscue Grid, marking any oral reading errors as appropriate. *Remember to count miscues only up to the point in the story containing the oral reading stop-marker (///).* Then complete the Developmental/Performance Summary to determine whether to continue the assessment. (*Note:* The Miscue Grid should be completed *after* the assessment session has been concluded in order to minimize stress for the student.)

ERROR TYPES · ERROR ANALYSIS

	mis-pronun.	sub-stitute	inser-tions	tchr. assist	omis-sions	Error Totals	Self-Correct.	(M) meaning	(S) Syntax	(V) Visual
Bears										
There are many kinds of bears.										
Some bears are brown. Others are										
black. Still others are white and										
are called polar bears. The biggest										
bears are called grizzly bears.										
Bears can smell and hear very										
well. Bears have small eyes and										
cannot see very well. They eat all										
kinds of food. They eat small animals,										
plants, and berries. Most bears sleep during										
the winter. When they wake up they										
are hungry. Bears can run very fast.										
They can climb trees. They are not safe										
animals to be around. The best place										
to be around bears is at the zoo. //										
TOTALS										

Summary of Reading Behaviors (Strengths and Needs)

PART III: MISCUE ANALYSIS

Directions: *Circle all reading behaviors you observed.*

A. Fundamental Behaviors Observed:

L → R Directionality   1 to 1 Matching   Searching for Clues   Cross-Checking

B. Word Attack Behaviors:

No Attempt   Mispronunciation (Invented word)   Substitutes

Skips/Reads On   Asks for Help   Repeats   Attempts to Self-Correct

"Sounds Out" (Segmenting)   Blends Sounds   Structural Analysis (Root words, Affixes)

C. Cueing Systems Used in Attempting Words

CUEING TOOL	MISCUE EXAMPLES	ACTUAL TEXT
(M) Meaning		
(S) Syntax		
(V) Visual		

D. Fluency (word by word → fluent reading)

Word by Word _____   Mixed Phrasing _____   Fluent Reading _____   Fluency Rate in Seconds _____

Performance Summary

Silent Reading Comprehension

_____ 0–1 questions missed = Easy

_____ 2 questions missed = Adequate

_____ 3+ questions missed = Too hard

Oral Reading Accuracy

_____ 0–1 oral error = Easy

_____ 2–5 oral errors = Adequate

_____ 6+ oral errors = Too hard

Continue to the next reading passage? _____ Yes   _____ No

ERROR TYPES — **ERROR ANALYSIS**

The Night Sky	mis-pronun.	sub-stitute	inser-tions	tchr. assist	omis-sions	Error Totals	Self-Correct.	(M) Meaning	(S) Syntax	(V) Visual
Look up at the sky at night. If it is a clear										
night, you will see stars. How many stars are										
there? No one knows for sure. But there										
is one star that you know by name. You										
can see it in the daytime. It is our sun.										
The sun is a star. All stars are suns.										
Our sun is so close that we cannot see										
other stars in the day. We only see										
the other suns at night. Stars are made										
up of very hot gas, and they seem to										
twinkle because of the air moving across										
them. Even // though we can't always see										
them, they are always in the sky,										
even in the daytime.										
TOTALS										

Summary of Reading Behaviors (Strengths and Needs)

PART III: MISCUE ANALYSIS

Directions: Circle all reading behaviors you observed.

A. Fundamental Behaviors Observed:

L → R Directionality   1 to 1 Matching   Searching for Clues   Cross-Checking

B. Word Attack Behaviors:

No Attempt   Mispronunciation (Invented word)   Substitutes

Skips/Reads On   Asks for Help   Repeats   Attempts to Self-Correct

"Sounds Out" (Segmenting)   Blends Sounds   Structural Analysis (Root words, Affixes)

C. Cueing Systems Used in Attempting Words

CUEING TOOL	MISCUE EXAMPLES	ACTUAL TEXT
(M) Meaning		
(S) Syntax		
(V) Visual		

D. Fluency (word by word → fluent reading)

Word by Word _____   Mixed Phrasing _____   Fluent Reading _____   Fluency Rate in Seconds _____

Performance Summary

Silent Reading Comprehension

_____ 0–1 questions missed = Easy

_____ 2 questions missed = Adequate

_____ 3+ questions missed = Too hard

Oral Reading Accuracy

_____ 0–1 oral error = Easy

_____ 2–5 oral errors = Adequate

_____ 6+ oral errors = Too hard

Continue to the next reading passage? _____ Yes   _____ No

PART IV: LISTENING COMPREHENSION

Directions: If you have decided not to continue to have the student read any other passages, then use this passage to begin assessing the student's listening comprehension (see page 19). Begin by reading the background statement for this passage and then say, "I am going to read this story to you. Please listen carefully because I will be asking you some questions after I finish reading it to you." After reading the passage, ask the student the questions associated with the passage. If the student correctly answers more than six questions, you will need to move to the next level and repeat the procedure.

Listening Comprehension

_____ 0–2 questions missed = move to the next passage level

_____ more than 2 questions missed = stop assessment or move down a level

Examiner's Notes:

C LEVEL 3 ASSESSMENT PROTOCOLS

Flying Flowers (194 words)

PART I: SILENT READING COMPREHENSION

Background Statement: "This selection is about a special kind of insect. It is about butterflies. Read this selection to find out some interesting facts about butterflies. I will ask you to tell me about what you read, so read carefully."

Teacher Directions: Once the student completes the silent reading, say, "Tell me about the story you just read." Answers to the questions below that the student provides during the retelling should be marked "ua" in the appropriate blank to indicate that this response was unaided. Ask all remaining questions not addressed during the retelling and mark those the student answers with an "a" to indicate that the correct response was given after prompting by the teacher.

*Questions/Answers
Element*

*Level of Comprehension/
Expository Grammar*

_____ 1. What kind of insect was the passage mainly about?
(*butterfly*)

literal/descriptive

_____ 2. Why is the butterfly referred to as the flying flower?
(*because of its many different colors*)

literal/collection

_____ 3. What gives the butterfly its colors?
(*scales*)

literal/causation

_____ 4. Can you name two ways in which a butterfly and
moth are different?
(*butterflies like the day, are more colorful, are thinner,
and most don't form cocoons—moths are the opposite*)

literal/comparison

_____ 5. Can you name two ways in which a butterfly and a
moth are alike?
(*they fly, lay eggs, have scales, have wings, etc.*)

inferential/comparison

_____ 6. What do antennae help a butterfly to do?
(*to smell and hear*)

literal/collection

_____ 7. Why do grown-up butterflies have to lay eggs as
soon as possible?
(*they don't live very long*)

inferential/problem-solution

_____ 8. What happens after a butterfly egg becomes a caterpillar?
(*it forms a hard skin that it has to break out of*)

literal/causation

PART II: ORAL READING AND ANALYSIS OF MISCUES

Directions: Say, "Now I would like to hear you read this story out loud." Have the student read orally until the 100-word sample is completed. Follow along on the Miscue Grid, marking any oral reading errors as appropriate. *Remember to count miscues only up to the point in the story containing the oral reading stop-marker (///).* Then complete the Developmental/Performance Summary to determine whether to continue the assessment. (*Note:* The Miscue Grid should be completed *after* the assessment session has been concluded in order to minimize stress for the student.)

ERROR TYPES   ERROR ANALYSIS

	mis-pronun.	sub-stitute	inser-tions	tchr. assist	omis-sions	Error Totals	Self-Correct.	(M) Meaning	(S) Syntax	(V) Visual
Flying Flowers										
There are many kinds of insects. There are										
big ones, little ones, ugly ones, biting ones,										
and helpful ones. But there is one kind of insect										
that most people agree is the most beautiful one.										
This insect is often called the flying flower.										
It is the butterfly. Butterflies are insects										
that have two pairs of wings. The wings										
are covered with tiny scales. These scales										
are different colors. These scales										
give the butterfly its beautiful colors.										
Butterflies smell and hear by using										
their long, thin antennae. Butterflies										
can't bite or chew. They use long,										
tube-like tongues to get at // *the food*										
they eat from flowers.										
TOTALS										

Summary of Reading Behaviors (Strengths and Needs)

PART III: MISCUE ANALYSIS

Directions: *Circle all reading behaviors you observed.*

A. Fundamental Behaviors Observed:

L → R Directionality   1 to 1 Matching   Searching for Clues   Cross-Checking

B. Word Attack Behaviors:

No Attempt   Mispronunciation (Invented word)   Substitutes

Skips/Reads On   Asks for Help   Repeats   Attempts to Self-Correct

"Sounds Out" (Segmenting)   Blends Sounds   Structural Analysis (Root words, Affixes)

C. Cueing Systems Used in Attempting Words

CUEING TOOL	MISCUE EXAMPLES	ACTUAL TEXT
(M) Meaning		
(S) Syntax		
(V) Visual		

D. Fluency (word by word → fluent reading)

Word by Word _____   Mixed Phrasing _____   Fluent Reading _____   Fluency Rate in Seconds _____

Performance Summary

Silent Reading Comprehension

_____ 0–1 questions missed = Easy

_____ 2 questions missed = Adequate

_____ 3+ questions missed = Too hard

Oral Reading Accuracy

_____ 0–1 oral error = Easy

_____ 2–5 oral errors = Adequate

_____ 6+ oral errors = Too hard

Continue to the next reading passage? _____ Yes   _____ No

PART IV: LISTENING COMPREHENSION

Directions: If you have decided not to continue to have the student read any other passages, then use this passage to begin assessing the student's listening comprehension (see page 19). Begin by reading the background statement for this passage and then say, "I am going to read this story to you. Please listen carefully because I will be asking you some questions after I finish reading it to you." After reading the passage, ask the student the questions associated with the passage. If the student correctly answers more than six questions, you will need to move to the next level and repeat the procedure.

Listening Comprehension

_____ 0–2 questions missed = move to the next passage level

_____ more than 2 questions missed = stop assessment or move down a level

Examiner's Notes:

LEVEL 4 ASSESSMENT PROTOCOLS

The Story of Coca-Cola (253 words)

PART I: SILENT READING COMPREHENSION

Background Statement: "This selection is about the history of Coca-Cola. Read it carefully and try to find out some facts about Coca-Cola, because I'm going to ask you to tell me about what you find."

Teacher Directions: Once the student completes the silent reading, say, "Tell me about the story you just read." Answers to the questions below that the student provides during the retelling should be marked "ua" in the appropriate blank to indicate that this response was unaided. Ask all remaining questions not addressed during the retelling and mark those the student answers with an "a" to indicate that the correct response was given after prompting by the teacher.

Questions/Answers

Level of Comprehension/ Expository Grammar Element

_____ 1. Who invented Coca-Cola?
   (*Mr./Dr. Pemberton*)

literal/causation

_____ 2. What was Dr. Pemberton trying to invent when he invented Coca-Cola?
   (*a headache medicine*)

literal/description

_____ 3. Besides drugs for headaches, what other things were put into Dr. Pemberton's new medicine?
   (*leaves, fruits, and nuts*)

literal/description

_____ 4. Why didn't the medicine sell very well at first?
   (*because the syrup was mixed with regular water*)

inferential/causation

_____ 5. Why could one say that Coca-Cola became popular because of a mistake?
   (*because a clerk accidentally mixed the syrup with carbonated water*)

inferential/problem-solution

_____ 6. In which city did the original Coca-Cola become a hit?
   (*Atlanta*)

literal/description

_____ 7. Explain what is different between today's Coca-Cola and the original version.
   (*no headache medicine, or other plausible responses*)

inferential/comparison

_____ 8. What's the difference between regular water and carbonated water?
   (*regular water doesn't have bubbles*)

inferential/comparison

PART II: ORAL READING AND ANALYSIS OF MISCUES

Directions: Say, "Now I would like to hear you read this story out loud." Have the student read orally until the 100-word sample is completed. Follow along on the Miscue Grid, marking any oral reading errors as appropriate. *Remember to count miscues only up to the point in the story containing the oral reading stop-marker (///).* Then complete the Developmental/Performance Summary to determine whether to continue the assessment. (*Note:* The Miscue Grid should be completed *after* the assessment session has been concluded in order to minimize stress for the student.)

ERROR TYPES | ERROR ANALYSIS

	mis-pronun.	sub-stitute	inser-tions	tchr. assist	omis-sions	Error Totals	Self-Correct.	(M) Meaning	(S) Syntax	(V) Visual
The Story of Coca-Cola										
Lots of people all over the world have heard										
of the soft drink called Coca-Cola. But not										
many people know the real story about										
how this drink was invented. Coca-Cola										
was the invention of a Mr. John Pemberton.										
Although he wasn't a doctor, most people										
called him Dr. Pemberton. He was a										
druggist in a town in the South. Dr.										
Pemberton liked to invent new things. He										
lived during the time just after the Civil										
War. One day Dr. Pemberton decided to										
make a headache medicine. He made it from										
nuts, fruits, and leaves. He also added										
the // *drugs necessary to cure a headache.*										
TOTALS										

Summary of Reading Behaviors (Strengths and Needs)

PART III: MISCUE ANALYSIS

Directions: *Circle all reading behaviors you observed.*

A. Fundamental Behaviors Observed:

L → R Directionality   1 to 1 Matching   Searching for Clues   Cross-Checking

B. Word Attack Behaviors:

No Attempt   Mispronunciation (Invented word)   Substitutes

Skips/Reads On   Asks for Help   Repeats   Attempts to Self-Correct

"Sounds Out" (Segmenting)   Blends Sounds   Structural Analysis (Root words, Affixes)

C. Cueing Systems Used in Attempting Words

CUEING TOOL	MISCUE EXAMPLES	ACTUAL TEXT
(M) Meaning		
(S) Syntax		
(V) Visual		

D. Fluency (word by word → fluent reading)

Word by Word _____   Mixed Phrasing _____   Fluent Reading _____   Fluency Rate in Seconds _____

Performance Summary

Silent Reading Comprehension

_____ 0–1 questions missed = Easy

_____ 2 questions missed = Adequate

_____ 3+ questions missed = Too hard

Oral Reading Accuracy

_____ 0–1 oral error = Easy

_____ 2–5 oral errors = Adequate

_____ 6+ oral errors = Too hard

Continue to the next reading passage? _____ Yes   _____ No

PART IV: LISTENING COMPREHENSION

Directions: If you have decided not to continue to have the student read any other passages, then use this passage to begin assessing the student's listening comprehension (see page 19). Begin by reading the background statement for this passage and then say, "I am going to read this story to you. Please listen carefully because I will be asking you some questions after I finish reading it to you." After reading the passage, ask the student the questions associated with the passage. If the student correctly answers more than six questions, you will need to move to the next level and repeat the procedure.

Listening Comprehension

_____ 0–2 questions missed = move to the next passage level

_____ more than 2 questions missed = stop assessment or move down a level

Examiner's Notes:

LEVEL 5 ASSESSMENT PROTOCOLS

Popcorn (282 words)

PART I: SILENT READING COMPREHENSION

Background Statement: "This selection is about corn, and *popcorn* in particular. Read the passage to discover some interesting facts about corn. Read it carefully because I'm going to ask you to tell me about what you read."

Teacher Directions: Once the student completes the silent reading, say, "Tell me about the story you just read." Answers to the questions below that the student provides during the retelling should be marked "ua" in the appropriate blank to indicate that this response was unaided. Ask all remaining questions not addressed during the retelling and mark those the student answers with an "a" to indicate that the correct response was given after prompting by the teacher.

Questions/Answers	*Level of Comprehension/ Expository Grammar Element*
_____ 1. Which type of corn is this passage mainly about? (*Indian corn or popcorn*)	inferential/descriptive
_____ 2. Explain how sweet corn differs from field corn. (*sweet corn is not used to feed livestock, tastes better, and has fuller kernels*)	inferential/comparison
_____ 3. What makes popcorn pop? (*water in the kernel*)	inferential/causation
_____ 4. What does the term *duds* mean when talking about popcorn? (*unpopped kernels*)	literal/description
_____ 5. Which of the methods to pop corn used by the Native Americans was the most effective, and why? (*the hot sand/clay bowl method because more kernels could be saved*)	inferential/problem-solution
_____ 6. How many pounds of popcorn did the passage say that the typical person in this country eats per year? (*two pounds*)	literal/description
_____ 7. How long did the passage say popcorn has been eaten by humans? (*thousands of years*)	literal/description
_____ 8. What is one limitation or problem associated with all three methods used by the Native Americans to pop corn? (*all lost kernels*)	inferential/problem-solution

PART II: ORAL READING AND ANALYSIS OF MISCUES

Directions: Say, "Now I would like to hear you read this story out loud." Have the student read orally until the 100-word sample is completed. Follow along on the Miscue Grid, marking any oral reading errors as appropriate. *Remember to count miscues only up to the point in the story containing the oral reading stop-marker (///).* Then complete the Developmental/Performance Summary to determine whether to continue the assessment. (*Note:* The Miscue Grid should be completed *after* the assessment session has been concluded in order to minimize stress for the student.)

ERROR TYPES

ERROR ANALYSIS

Popcorn	mis-pronun.	sub-stitute	inser-tions	tchr. assist	omis-sions	Error Totals	Self-Correct.	(M) Meaning	(S) Syntax	(V) Visual
There are three major types of corn grown										
in this country. First, there is the type of										
corn people eat most of the time. It is										
called sweet corn because of its flavor.										
Second, there is field corn, which is										
used mainly for feeding livestock.										
Sometimes people eat field corn too.										
However, its taste is not as good as sweet										
corn and its kernels are not as full. The										
third type of corn, often called Indian										
corn, is popcorn. Popcorn is grown										
commercially in the United States because										
the average American eats almost two										
pounds of popcorn a year, according //										
to various estimates.										
TOTALS										

Summary of Reading Behaviors (Strengths and Needs)

PART III: MISCUE ANALYSIS

Directions: *Circle all reading behaviors you observed.*

A. Fundamental Behaviors Observed:

L → R Directionality   1 to 1 Matching   Searching for Clues   Cross-Checking

B. Word Attack Behaviors:

No Attempt   Mispronunciation (Invented word)   Substitutes

Skips/Reads On   Asks for Help   Repeats   Attempts to Self-Correct

"Sounds Out" (Segmenting)   Blends Sounds   Structural Analysis (Root words, Affixes)

C. Cueing Systems Used in Attempting Words

CUEING TOOL	MISCUE EXAMPLES	ACTUAL TEXT
(M) Meaning		
(S) Syntax		
(V) Visual		

D. Fluency (word by word → fluent reading)

Word by Word _____   Mixed Phrasing _____   Fluent Reading _____   Fluency Rate in Seconds _____

Performance Summary

Silent Reading Comprehension

_____ 0–1 questions missed = Easy

_____ 2 questions missed = Adequate

_____ 3+ questions missed = Too hard

Oral Reading Accuracy

_____ 0–1 oral error = Easy

_____ 2–5 oral errors = Adequate

_____ 6+ oral errors = Too hard

Continue to the next reading passage? _____ Yes   _____ No

PART IV: LISTENING COMPREHENSION

Directions: If you have decided not to continue to have the student read any other passages, then use this passage to begin assessing the student's listening comprehension (see page 19). Begin by reading the background statement for this passage and then say, "I am going to read this story to you. Please listen carefully because I will be asking you some questions after I finish reading it to you." After reading the passage, ask the student the questions associated with the passage. If the student correctly answers more than six questions, you will need to move to the next level and repeat the procedure.

Listening Comprehension

_____ 0–2 questions missed = move to the next passage level

_____ more than 2 questions missed = stop assessment or move down a level

Examiner's Notes:

LEVEL 6 ASSESSMENT PROTOCOLS

Cooking Without Fire: The Microwave Oven (219 words)

PART I: SILENT READING COMPREHENSION

Background Statement: "This passage is about microwave ovens. Read the selection to find out how microwave ovens were developed. Read it carefully because I'm going to ask you to tell me about what you read."

Teacher Directions: Once the student completes the silent reading, say, "Tell me about the story you just read." Answers to the questions below that the student provides during the retelling should be marked "ua" in the appropriate blank to indicate that this response was unaided. Ask all remaining questions not addressed during the retelling and mark those the student answers with an "a" to indicate that the correct response was given after prompting by the teacher.

Questions/Answers

Level of Comprehension/Expository Grammar Element

_____ 1. What invention led to the development of the microwave oven?
(*magnetron tube*)

literal/causation

_____ 2. For what job was the magnetron tube first used?
(*radar*)

literal/description

_____ 3. What did Dr. Percy Spencer discover about the magnetron tube?
(*it could heat food from the inside out*)

literal/description

_____ 4. What was the name given to the first microwave oven?
(*Radar Range*)

literal/description

_____ 5. Name two ways that today's microwave ovens differ from the first ones.
(*not as bulky, more features, less expensive*)

literal/comparison

_____ 6. Explain why some people consider microwave cooking the first new method of cooking since the discovery of fire.
(*it requires no fire or element of fire to cook food*)

literal/causation

_____ 7. What type of energy is used by the microwave to cook food?
(*electromagnetic*)

literal/description

_____ 8. What are two features found on most microwave ovens, according to the passage?
(*defrost, reheat, constant temperature cooking*)

literal/description

PART II: ORAL READING AND ANALYSIS OF MISCUES

Directions: Say, "Now I would like to hear you read this story out loud." Have the student read orally until the 100-word sample is completed. Follow along on the Miscue Grid, marking any oral reading errors as appropriate. *Remember to count miscues only up to the point in the story containing the oral reading stop-marker (///).* Then complete the Developmental/Performance Summary to determine whether to continue the assessment. (*Note:* The Miscue Grid should be completed *after* the assessment session has been concluded in order to minimize stress for the student.)

Cooking Without Fire: The Microwave Oven

	mis-pronun.	sub-stitute	inser-tions	tchr. assist	omis-sions	Error Totals	Self-Correct.	(M) Meaning	(S) Syntax	(V) Visual
Microwave cooking is very common today. It										
is, however, a recent invention. The microwave										
oven one uses today was developed from the										
invention of the magnetron tube in 1940. The										
invention of the magnetron tube, by Sir John										
Randall and Dr. H. A. Boot, was a very important										
part of the radar defense of England during										
World War II. Neither man considered it as a										
means of preparing food after they invented it. It										
wasn't until the late 1940s that Dr. Percy										
Spencer discovered the magnetron's ability to										
heat and cook food from the inside out. Spencer										
experimented with many different // foods, all										
with the same results: The inside got hot first.										
TOTALS										

Summary of Reading Behaviors (Strengths and Needs)

PART III: MISCUE ANALYSIS

Directions: *Circle all reading behaviors you observed.*

A. Fundamental Behaviors Observed:

L → R Directionality   1 to 1 Matching   Searching for Clues   Cross-Checking

B. Word Attack Behaviors:

No Attempt   Mispronunciation (Invented word)   Substitutes

Skips/Reads On   Asks for Help   Repeats   Attempts to Self-Correct

"Sounds Out" (Segmenting)   Blends Sounds   Structural Analysis (Root words, Affixes)

C. Cueing Systems Used in Attempting Words

CUEING TOOL	MISCUE EXAMPLES	ACTUAL TEXT
(M) Meaning		
(S) Syntax		
(V) Visual		

D. Fluency (word by word → fluent reading)

Word by Word _____   Mixed Phrasing _____   Fluent Reading _____   Fluency Rate in Seconds _____

Performance Summary

Silent Reading Comprehension

_____ 0–1 questions missed = Easy

_____ 2 questions missed = Adequate

_____ 3+ questions missed = Too hard

Oral Reading Accuracy

_____ 0–1 oral error = Easy

_____ 2–5 oral errors = Adequate

_____ 6+ oral errors = Too hard

Continue to the next reading passage? _____ Yes   _____ No

PART IV: LISTENING COMPREHENSION

Directions: If you have decided not to continue to have the student read any other passages, then use this passage to begin assessing the student's listening comprehension (see page 19). Begin by reading the background statement for this passage and then say, "I am going to read this story to you. Please listen carefully because I will be asking you some questions after I finish reading it to you." After reading the passage, ask the student the questions associated with the passage. If the student correctly answers more than six questions, you will need to move to the next level and repeat the procedure.

Listening Comprehension

_____ 0–2 questions missed = move to the next passage level

_____ more than 2 questions missed = stop assessment or move down a level

Examiner's Notes:

LEVEL 7 ASSESSMENT PROTOCOLS

Diamonds (286 words)

PART I: SILENT READING COMPREHENSION

Background Statement: "The following selection is about diamonds. Read it carefully to find out about how diamonds are made, because I'm going to ask you to tell me all about what you read."

Teacher Directions: Once the student completes the silent reading, say, "Tell me about the story you just read." Answers to the questions below that the student provides during the retelling should be marked "ua" in the appropriate blank to indicate that this response was unaided. Ask all remaining questions not addressed during the retelling and mark those the student answers with an "a" to indicate that the correct response was given after prompting by the teacher.

Questions/Answers	*Level of Comprehension/ Expository Grammar Element*
_____ 1. Where are the most important diamond fields located? (*India, South America, and Africa*)	literal/description
_____ 2. What information in the passage supports the idea that diamonds are rare? (*only located in certain areas, and even when present tons of rock must be sorted through*)	inferential/problem-solution
_____ 3. Where were the first diamonds found? (*sand and gravel in stream beds*)	literal/description
_____ 4. What four things determine the quality of a diamond? (*purity, color, weight, and cut*)	literal/description
_____ 5. What causes the brilliance of a diamond? (*the way it is cut, or number of facets*)	literal/causation
_____ 6. What two factors lower the purity of a diamond? (*uncrystallized carbon and foreign substances*)	inferential/causation
_____ 7. Explain how artificial diamonds are made. (*they result from carbon being placed under high pressure and temperature*)	inferential/collection
_____ 8. Describe where natural diamonds are found. (*in rock formations that look like volcanoes*)	literal/description

PART II: ORAL READING AND ANALYSIS OF MISCUES

Directions: Say, "Now I would like to hear you read this story out loud." Have the student read orally until the 100-word sample is completed. Follow along on the Miscue Grid, marking any oral reading errors as appropriate. *Remember to count miscues only up to the point in the story containing the oral reading stop-marker (//).* Then complete the Developmental/Performance Summary to determine whether to continue the assessment. (*Note:* The Miscue Grid should be completed *after* the assessment session has been concluded in order to minimize stress for the student.)

ERROR TYPES | ERROR ANALYSIS

	mis-pronun.	sub-stitute	inser-tions	tchr. assist	omis-sions	Error Totals	Self-Correct.	(M) Meaning	(S) Syntax	(V) Visual
Diamonds										
A diamond is one of the most beautiful										
treasures that nature ever created, and one										
of the rarest. It takes thousands of years										
for nature to transform a chunk of carbon										
into a rough diamond. Only three important										
diamond fields have been found in the										
world—in India, South America, and Africa.										
The first diamonds were found in the sand										
and gravel of stream beds. These types of										
diamonds are called alluvial diamonds.										
Later, diamonds were found deep in										
the earth in rock formations called pipes.										
These formations resemble extinct volcanos.										
The rock in which diamonds are found is										
called // *blue ground.*										
TOTALS										

Summary of Reading Behaviors (Strengths and Needs)

PART III: MISCUE ANALYSIS

Directions: Circle all reading behaviors you observed.

A. Fundamental Behaviors Observed:

L → R Directionality   1 to 1 Matching   Searching for Clues   Cross-Checking

B. Word Attack Behaviors:

No Attempt   Mispronunciation (Invented word)   Substitutes

Skips/Reads On   Asks for Help   Repeats   Attempts to Self-Correct

"Sounds Out" (Segmenting)   Blends Sounds   Structural Analysis (Root words, Affixes)

C. Cueing Systems Used in Attempting Words

CUEING TOOL	MISCUE EXAMPLES	ACTUAL TEXT
(M) Meaning		
(S) Syntax		
(V) Visual		

D. Fluency (word by word → fluent reading)

Word by Word _____   Mixed Phrasing _____   Fluent Reading _____   Fluency Rate in Seconds _____

Performance Summary

Silent Reading Comprehension

_____ 0–1 questions missed = Easy

_____ 2 questions missed = Adequate

_____ 3+ questions missed = Too hard

Oral Reading Accuracy

_____ 0–1 oral error = Easy

_____ 2–5 oral errors = Adequate

_____ 6+ oral errors = Too hard

Continue to the next reading passage? _____ Yes   _____ No

PART IV: LISTENING COMPREHENSION

Directions: If you have decided not to continue to have the student read any other passages, then use this passage to begin assessing the student's listening comprehension (see page 19). Begin by reading the background statement for this passage and then say, "I am going to read this story to you. Please listen carefully because I will be asking you some questions after I finish reading it to you." After reading the passage, ask the student the questions associated with the passage. If the student correctly answers more than six questions, you will need to move to the next level and repeat the procedure.

Listening Comprehension

_____ 0–2 questions missed = move to the next passage level

_____ more than 2 questions missed = stop assessment or move down a level

Examiner's Notes:

LEVEL 8 ASSESSMENT PROTOCOLS

The Future Is Here (375 words)

PART I: SILENT READING COMPREHENSION

Background Statement: "This selection is about some inventions that will affect people in the near future. Read it carefully to find out what some of the inventions are and the ways they will affect people because I'm going to ask you to tell me about what you read."

Teacher Directions: Once the student completes the silent reading, say, "Tell me about the story you just read." Answers to the questions below that the student provides during the retelling should be marked "ua" in the appropriate blank to indicate that this response was unaided. Ask all remaining questions not addressed during the retelling and mark those the student answers with an "a" to indicate that the correct response was given after prompting by the teacher.

Questions/Answers

*Level of Comprehension/
Expository Grammar Element*

_____ 1. What is a levitation vehicle?
(*a machine that is part aircraft and part car*)

inferential/collection

_____ 2. Why are people working on this type of vehicle?
(*crowded highways and increase in population*)

literal/causation

_____ 3. Explain how a dental laser works.
(*a laser destroys the cavity without pain*)

inferential/causation

_____ 4. Explain why a full-motion, color video telephone
will benefit the deaf.
(*the deaf will be able to call people who know sign
language and communicate with them*)

inferential/causation

_____ 5. What do fiber optics do that traditional technology is
unable to do?
(*allow communication of lots of information over
very thin wires*)

inferential/comparison

_____ 6. What two areas of your current television will be
upgraded when high-definition TV becomes common?
(*sound and picture*)

literal/description

_____ 7. What does the sound and picture quality of high-definition
TV compare to?
(*compact discs and 35-millimeter movies*)

literal/comparison

_____ 8. What did the passage say about how new advancements
will affect people?
(*responses will vary but should relate to helping people meet
the challenges of the future*)

inferential/causation

PART II: ORAL READING AND ANALYSIS OF MISCUES

Directions: Say, "Now I would like to hear you read this story out loud." Have the student read orally until the 100-word sample is completed. Follow along on the Miscue Grid, marking any oral reading errors as appropriate. *Remember to count miscues only up to the point in the story containing the oral reading stop-marker (///).* Then complete the Developmental/Performance Summary to determine whether to continue the assessment. (*Note:* The Miscue Grid should be completed *after* the assessment session has been concluded in order to minimize stress for the student.)

ERROR ANALYSIS

	(M) Meaning	(S) Syntax	(V) Visual

ERROR TYPES

	mis-pronun.	sub-stitute	inser-tions	tchr. assist	omis-sions	Error Totals	Self-Correct.
The Future Is Here							
What will the twenty-first century bring							
in terms of new inventions and space-age							
technologies? No one knows for sure. But							
scientists, inventors, and futurists are predicting							
a variety of new inventions. These new							
advancements will affect the way we live							
and play. Some of them are already on the							
drawing board. One example is the levitation							
vehicle. The idea of a vertical take-off and							
landing aircraft that can also be driven on							
the road is the invention of Paul Moeller.							
He named his first version of this type of							
craft the Moeller 400. People involved in							
this // type of technology see increases in							
population and crowded highways as reasons							
that a levitation vehicle will be needed.							
TOTALS							

Summary of Reading Behaviors (Strengths and Needs)

PART III: MISCUE ANALYSIS

Directions: *Circle all reading behaviors you observed.*

A. Fundamental Behaviors Observed:

L → R Directionality   1 to 1 Matching   Searching for Clues   Cross-Checking

B. Word Attack Behaviors:

No Attempt   Mispronunciation (Invented word)   Substitutes

Skips/Reads On   Asks for Help   Repeats   Attempts to Self-Correct

"Sounds Out" (Segmenting)   Blends Sounds   Structural Analysis (Root words, Affixes)

C. Cueing Systems Used in Attempting Words

CUEING TOOL	MISCUE EXAMPLES	ACTUAL TEXT
(M) Meaning		
(S) Syntax		
(V) Visual		

D. Fluency (word by word → fluent reading)

Word by Word _____   Mixed Phrasing _____   Fluent Reading _____   Fluency Rate in Seconds _____

Performance Summary

Silent Reading Comprehension

_____ 0–1 questions missed = Easy

_____ 2 questions missed = Adequate

_____ 3+ questions missed = Too hard

Oral Reading Accuracy

_____ 0–1 oral error = Easy

_____ 2–5 oral errors = Adequate

_____ 6+ oral errors = Too hard

Continue to the next reading passage? _____ Yes   _____ No

PART IV: LISTENING COMPREHENSION

Directions: If you have decided not to continue to have the student read any other passages, then use this passage to begin assessing the student's listening comprehension (see page 19). Begin by reading the background statement for this passage and then say, "I am going to read this story to you. Please listen carefully because I will be asking you some questions after I finish reading it to you." After reading the passage, ask the student the questions associated with the passage. If the student correctly answers more than six questions, you will need to move to the next level and repeat the procedure.

Listening Comprehension

_____ 0–2 questions missed = move to the next passage level

_____ more than 2 questions missed = stop assessment or move down a level

Examiner's Notes:

LEVEL 9 ASSESSMENT PROTOCOLS

Visual Illusions (269 words)

PART I: SILENT READING COMPREHENSION

Background Statement: "This selection is about visual illusions. Read it to find out about three specific types of visual illusions. Read it carefully because when you finish I will ask you to tell me about what you have read."

Teacher Directions: Once the student completes the silent reading, say, "Tell me about the story you just read." Answers to the questions below that the student provides during the retelling should be marked "ua" in the appropriate blank to indicate that this response was unaided. Ask all remaining questions not addressed during the retelling and mark those the student answers with an "a" to indicate that the correct response was given after prompting by the teacher.

Questions/Answers

Level of Comprehension/ Expository Grammar Element

_____ 1. What two reasons were given for visual illusions?
   (*preconceptions and the brain's difficulty in choosing from two or more patterns*)

literal/description

_____ 2. What is an example of a lateral inhibition illusion?
   (*a bull's-eye*)

literal/description

_____ 3. The Gateway Arch in St. Louis is an example of what distortion?
   (*length distortion*)

literal/description

_____ 4. Explain why length distortion occurs.
   (*because the eyes work better side to side than up and down*)

literal/collection

_____ 5. What's an example of the visual illusion called "Hermann's Grid"?
   (*modern buildings*)

literal/description

_____ 6. How does Hermann's Grid affect what you see visually?
   (*it causes the eyes to see gray spots at the corners of squares*)

inferential/causation

_____ 7. Explain why the old axiom "Don't believe everything you see" is valid in everyday life.
   (*examples of visual illusions are all around us, or other plausible responses*)

inferential/collection

_____ 8. How does the tendency of eyes to move more easily from side to side rather than up and down affect the way we perceive tall objects?
   (*they seem taller than they actually are*)

literal/causation

PART II: ORAL READING AND ANALYSIS OF MISCUES

Directions: Say, "Now I would like to hear you read this story out loud." Have the student read orally until the 100-word sample is completed. Follow along on the Miscue Grid, marking any oral reading errors as appropriate. *Remember to count miscues only up to the point in the story containing the oral reading stop-marker (//).* Then complete the Developmental/Performance Summary to determine whether to continue the assessment. (*Note:* The Miscue Grid should be completed *after* the assessment session has been concluded in order to minimize stress for the student.)

Visual Illusions

	mis-pronun.	sub-stitute	inser-tions	tchr. assist	omis-sions	Error Totals	Self-Correct.	(M) Meaning	(S) Syntax	(V) Visual
A visual illusion is an unreal or misleading										
appearance of image, according to *Webster's*										
dictionary. In other words, visual illusions are										
sometimes caused by ideas one holds about										
what one expects to see. In other instances,										
the illusion is caused by the brain's difficulty										
in choosing from two or more visual patterns.										
If you look at a bull's-eye and move it										
slowly in circular motions, you should see										
spokes moving. The spokes, if you see them,										
aren't really there. This type of visual illusion is										
called lateral inhibition. Another type of										
visual illusion occurs when a person tries										
to // *estimate the height of a vertical object.*										
TOTALS										

Summary of Reading Behaviors (Strengths and Needs)

PART III: MISCUE ANALYSIS

Directions: *Circle all reading behaviors you observed.*

A. Fundamental Behaviors Observed:

L → R Directionality   1 to 1 Matching   Searching for Clues   Cross-Checking

B. Word Attack Behaviors:

No Attempt   Mispronunciation (Invented word)   Substitutes

Skips/Reads On   Asks for Help   Repeats   Attempts to Self-Correct

"Sounds Out" (Segmenting)   Blends Sounds   Structural Analysis (Root words, Affixes)

C. Cueing Systems Used in Attempting Words

CUEING TOOL	MISCUE EXAMPLES	ACTUAL TEXT
(M) Meaning		
(S) Syntax		
(V) Visual		

D. Fluency (word by word → fluent reading)

Word by Word _____   Mixed Phrasing _____   Fluent Reading _____   Fluency Rate in Seconds _____

Performance Summary

Silent Reading Comprehension

_____ 0–1 questions missed = Easy

_____ 2 questions missed = Adequate

_____ 3+ questions missed = Too hard

Oral Reading Accuracy

_____ 0–1 oral error = Easy

_____ 2–5 oral errors = Adequate

_____ 6+ oral errors = Too hard

Continue to the next reading passage? _____ Yes   _____ No

FORM D: LEVEL 1

1. Dogs can bark.

2. Cats can be friends.

3. There are many kinds of animals.

FORM D: LEVEL 2

1. Look at things in your bedroom.

2. These shapes have color.

3. Purple is made by mixing other colors.

FORM D: LEVEL 3

1. Some books are interesting.

2. It had not been invented.

3. He allowed the book to be read over.

FORM D: LEVEL 4

1. They trapped animals in the mountains.

2. He lived in unknown parts of the country.

3. He discovered a pass out West.

FORM D: LEVEL 5

1. Mexico lies south of the United States.

2. Some music is played with violins.

3. Guitar music is unique when played in a group.

FORM D: LEVEL 6

1. Some laws still discriminate against people.

2. Celebrations were held for the national hero.

3. A stormy argument took place.

FORM D: LEVEL 7

1. There are literally hundreds of measurements.

2. They frequently are pointed or barbed to make for better fastening.

3. The profession usually uses a gauge to determine a product's value.

FORM D: LEVEL 8

1. The continent is home to a large population.

2. There was not suitable soil in the central part of the region.

3. The grassland was a fascinating place to visit.

FORM D: LEVEL 9

1. The amount of cholesterol in your diet can affect your health.

2. There is a myriad of ways to monitor your caloric intake.

3. The continuum provides a wide range of nutritional options.

EXPOSITORY PASSAGES

Animal Friends

There are many kinds of animals.
Some animals are our friends. Others are not.
Dogs and cats can be good friends.

Dogs and cats make sounds to talk to us.
Some dogs bark when they hear something.
Some dogs bark when they are hungry.
Cats purr when they are happy.
Cats meow when they are hungry.

Not all cats and dogs are your friends.
If you do not know a dog, do not pet it.
It might bite you.
Cats can hurt you too.
Cats have claws and they can bite.

Making Pictures Is Art

Look around and you can see art everywhere.
Look at things in your bedroom. They all have
lines, shape, and color. People who do art, or
artists, use lines, shape, and color to make pictures.

Lines can be thick or thin. Lines can be short or
long. You would need to use lines to draw your
face. Lines are used to make shapes. In your room
at home, your bed, night light, and wall have
shape. These things also have color.

Red, yellow, and blue are the main colors.
All other colors can be made by mixing these colors.
Orange is made by mixing red and yellow.
Green is made by mixing yellow and blue.
Purple is made by mixing red and blue.
Black and white are not colors.
They do not have blue, yellow, or red in them.

The History of Books

The history of books is interesting. A long time ago most people could not read. The people who could read didn't have many books to read. They didn't have many books because the printing press had not been invented. All books had to be hand written on either an animal skin or a kind of paper.

Most books were written on stretched sheepskin or stretched calfskin. The cost of writing a book on skin limited how many could be made. Only the rich could own books. Most books were written on skins because they were stronger and prettier than those written on paper. Hundreds of years ago it could have taken a whole flock of sheep to make one book because it took one sheepskin for each page.

The invention of the printing press changed the world. The printing press allowed many more books to be made. As books became more common, many people began to learn how to read. For the first time, books began to be used to teach people about art, science, and faraway places. No longer were people required to remember everything. They could read about the world in books over and over again if they chose to do so.

Mountain Man

During the early history of our country, the West was full of stories about cowboys and Indians. Another group that helped settle the West were the mountain men. These were men who wanted to trap animals for their furs. These men went into unknown parts of the West beyond the Rocky Mountains. They carried a gun, a knife, coffee, flour, and little else. They planned to eat the animals they shot and the berries they found. They went to trap beaver for their furs. Some of these men made friends with the Indians who lived in the far West. Others did not. One famous mountain man who made friends with the Indians was Jim Beckwourth.

Jim Beckwourth was a black man. He had been a slave. At the age of 20 he decided he didn't want to be a slave. He ran away. He made it to the Rocky Mountains and became a mountain man. Jim began trapping and made friends with the local Indian tribe called the Crow. Jim married an Indian woman. He even became a chief of the Crows. Later on, Jim decided he needed to move further west. He headed off for California and discovered a pass through the mountains to California. The pass through the mountains still bears his name today. Jim Beckwourth couldn't read or write but he got his story written down. His story is in a book called *The Life and Adventures of James P. Beckwourth.*

Music of Mexico

Much of the music you hear in the United States comes from other countries. Most people who come to the United States from other countries adapt to the lifestyle here. However, they do not give up the music of their homelands.

Many people have come to the United States from Mexico. Mexico is a large country that lies south of the United States. The music of Mexico is unique and has contributed much to the music heard in the United States. Music from Mexico often uses instruments such as the folk harp, violin, and various types of guitars.

Music in Mexico is used to celebrate birthdays, weddings, anniversaries, and other holidays. The people like music and they show it. They sing along with the musicians and often burst out with yells, laughter, clapping, and dancing.

Two types of music that are popular throughout Mexico are from states in the east and west. In the east, music is performed on four instruments. A band in the east generally has a 35-string harp that plays the melody and bass, a thin guitar, a six-string guitar, and a four-string guitar. The music is lively and fast paced. A famous song from this part of Mexico is La Bamba. Music from the western part of Mexico is usually played by a musical group. These musical groups called "mariachi" (mah-ree-AH-chee) play many types of music. The group usually consists of several violins, two trumpets, a large bass guitar, a short five-string guitar, and a six-string guitar. Mariachi often play for special events. Other times mariachi can be seen strolling along the street playing and singing to people eating or shopping.

Jesse Owens

In 1936, the Olympic games were to be held in Germany. For months before the games took place, a stormy argument took place in the United States. Germany was ruled by Adolf Hitler and the Nazi Party. Hitler had been mistreating German Jews for some time, and many people in the United States wondered whether we should send a team or stay home and protest German racism. It was finally decided that we should send a team.

At the same time, many black athletes wondered if they should go because of racism in the United States. Finally, led by Jesse Owens, the black American athletes decided they should go to Germany to show the Germans how great they were. Jesse Owens led the American team to victory by capturing four Gold Medals. Jesse returned home a national hero. Many cities held parades and celebrations in his honor. Yet in much of the United States, laws still discriminated against black citizens.

In his later life, Jesse Owens, without bitterness, wrote the following. "In the early 1830s my ancestors were brought on a boat across the Atlantic Ocean from Africa to America as slaves for men who felt they had the right to own other men. In August of 1936, I boarded a boat to go back across the Atlantic Ocean to do battle with Adolf Hitler, a man who thought all other men should be slave to him and his armies."

Jesse Owens's Gold Medals did little to stop the direction of Germany in 1936. However, they did help move the United States a step closer toward providing equal treatment for all Americans regardless of their race.

Nails: A Carpenter's "Fastener"

Carpenters use a variety of tools in their profession such as hammers, saws, and power tools. They also use what are called *fasteners* to hold pieces of wood and other materials together. The most widely used fasteners are nails, screws, and bolts. Nails are perhaps the most commonly used fasteners in the carpenter's toolbox.

There are literally hundreds of kinds of nails that can be used for just about any kind of fastening job. The size of nails is usually designated using the *penny system*. While we are not exactly sure how the penny system came about, many people believe that it is an ancient measurement based on the price of nails according to weight per one hundred nails. Larger and heavier nails would cost more pennies than smaller nails, thus a six penny nail (written as "6d") would cost more than a two penny (2d) nail. In the penny system, the smallest nail is a two-penny (2d) nail and the largest is a sixty-penny (60d) nail. The thickness or *gauge* of nails usually increases as nails get longer, so a 50d nail will typically be much thicker in gauge than a 10d nail.

There are many ways of making nails, and each type is better suited to different purposes. One type of nail that is not used very often is called the *cut* nail. Cut nails are given that name because they are literally cut or *stamped* from thin metal sheets and are wedge-shaped.

Wire nails are cut from long rolls of metal wire and most often come in three types: common, box, and finish nails. *Common nails* have a smooth shaft, are of fairly heavy gauge, and have a medium-sized head. They frequently have a pointed or barbed section under the head to improve holding power and make for better fastening. *Box nails* are very much like common nails except they are much thinner (smaller gauge). This makes them better suited to fastening edges of wood with less danger of splitting the wood. *Finish nails* are light gauge (very thin) and are ideal for what is called "finishing work" on the inside of homes. They have a small head and can be driven into the wood so as to become almost invisible.

An old saying among carpenters is "always use the right tool for the right job." Knowing just which nail is the correct fastening tool is one way master carpenters live up to this important motto.

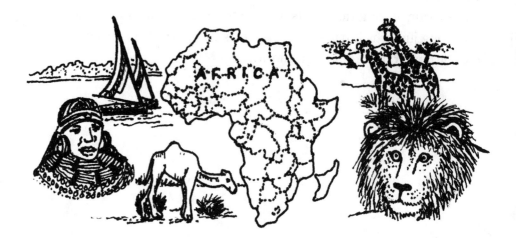

The Environments of Africa

Africa is the Earth's second largest continent. It is home to about one-tenth of the world population. While it is about three times larger than the United States in terms of landmass, many people still do not know very much about it. Some think of Africa as a single country and it is not. In this selection we take a brief tour of this continent.

Africa is almost completely surrounded by water. Two oceans and two seas are on her borders. The Atlantic Ocean borders Africa on the east, while the Indian Ocean borders to the west. The Mediterranean Sea and the Red Sea are to the north. The famous Sahara Desert stretches across Africa. It separates North African countries from the southern countries, which are often called sub-Saharan Africa. As of the 1990s, there were some 49 countries in sub-Saharan Africa alone. Because the equator runs through sub-Saharan Africa, most of this region has a climate that is quite warm and moist or *tropical*.

Central and West African countries are thinly populated because of a lack of suitable soil for farming. They do, however, have many tropical rain forests, which are of great benefit to people around the Earth. A major concern to many is that these splendid rain forests are being cut down to make way for farming and houses. Among other things, the loss of the rain forests leads to a great deal of soil erosion and the loss of plant and animal habitats.

As we move further away from the equator, we find that the African rain forests disappear and are replaced by grasslands known as *savannas*. In East Africa, there are thick grasslands where large herds of big game animals such as the giraffe, antelope, and zebra roam. Farming is also an important way of life in these East Africa countries.

The *African Horn* is also part of East Africa and bulges out into the Indian Ocean. It is a mass of hills, mountains, canyons, and valleys that slope down toward the dry lowlands near the Red Sea. Because of overpopulation and other problems, there is a great deal of poverty in this region. The African Horn is home to four countries: Ethiopia, Somalia, Eritrea, and Djibouti.

Southern Africa is a fascinating place that features wooded areas to the north and, because of less rainfall, grasslands to the south. Some of the countries located in Southern Africa include Angola, Zambia, Namibia, and South Africa. There has been a great deal of political change in South Africa over the last twenty years as this country moved from government ruled by white citizens only to a democracy that allows everyone to vote for her leaders.

Finally, as we travel to North Africa above the Sahara Desert, we see that it is home to such ancient countries as Egypt, Sudan, Libya, Algeria, and Morocco. These nations have their own special character and traditions that can vary greatly from their African neighbors to the south. Without doubt, Africa is a continent rich in traditions, culture, and varied geography.

The Mathematics of Health

Americans spend billions of dollars every year on medical care. Doctor bills, medicine, dental work, optical products (glasses, contacts, etc.), health insurance, nursing homes, and other health-related costs are all part of the health care picture. As the associated costs of medical care continue to escalate, more and more Americans are making efforts to stay healthy in a myriad of ways. These efforts range on a continuum from daily exercise to careful control of one's diet. This passage will focus on the mathematics involved in monitoring one's diet.

People sometimes try to remain healthy by limiting the amount of fat, sodium (salt), cholesterol, and sugar in their diet. Too much fat in your diet, for instance, can lead to heart disease and other deadly health problems. Years ago many food producers began marketing products carrying labels like *LITE* (low in fat or sugar) or *Lo-Cal* (low in calories) to suggest that their foods were more healthy than some of their competitors' products. Sometimes, however, these food products were not any more healthy than their competitors that did not carry the LITE or Lo-Cal markings.

In 1994, the federal Food and Drug Administration (FDA) in Washington, D.C., created new rules for food producers marking their products "LITE," "Lo-Cal," or "Light." Now all companies, except for the very smallest, must provide nutritional information on their labels for consumers so that we can judge for ourselves whether the food is as low in fat, sodium, cholesterol, or sugar as we expect.

Sometimes when we are shopping for groceries, it can be interesting to compare products just to see how much fat is contained in them. This can help us to choose foods that are as healthy as they are pleasing to the taste. For example, a frankfurter typically has about thirteen grams of fat (*Note:* This is written as "13g" on the label next to where it says "Fat"). Roast turkey, on the other hand, has 12.5g *less* fat than a frankfurter! Here is another example. A can of orange soda has about 110 calories, mostly due to the amount of sugar it contains. However, a LITE or diet soda only has about one calorie. If a grown person should usually consume about 1500 calories per day from all foods, think of how many calories can be saved for other more pleasing foods just by switching to a diet soda without sugar.

Becoming a "label reader" can be a great way to add years to your life while also helping you enjoy the foods you eat. Maybe, as the old saying goes, "You *can* have your cake and eat it, too!" as long as you pay close attention to *what* you put into the cake.

EXAMINER'S
ASSESSMENT PROTOCOLS

LEVEL 1 ASSESSMENT PROTOCOLS

Animal Friends (91 words)

PART I: SILENT READING COMPREHENSION

Background Statement: "This story is about dogs and cats. Read it and try to remember some of the important facts about these animals because I'm going to ask you to tell me about what you have read."

Teacher Directions: Once the student completes the silent reading, say, "Tell me about the story you just read." Answers to the questions below that the student provides during the retelling should be marked "ua" in the appropriate blank to indicate that this response was unaided. Ask all remaining questions not addressed during the retelling and mark those student answers with an "a" to indicate that the correct response was given after prompting by the teacher.

Questions/Answers

Level of Comprehension/ Expository Grammar Element

_____ 1. What two kinds of animals were in this story?
(*dogs and cats*)

literal/description

_____ 2. Why do cats purr?
(*they are happy*)

literal/description

_____ 3. What were the two reasons given for dogs barking?
(*hungry and when they hear something*)

literal/collection

_____ 4. Why is it best not to pet a dog you do not know?
(*it might bite you*)

literal/problem-solution

_____ 5. What two ways can a cat hurt someone?
(*scratch or bite*)

literal/collection

_____ 6. What do cats do when they are hungry?
(*meow*)

literal/description

_____ 7. What does "dogs and cats like to talk to us" mean?
(*It means that when they bark or meow or make other noises, they are trying to let people know they hear something, are hungry, or happy*)

inferential/causation

_____ 8. Can you think of any animals that aren't our friends?
(*accept plausible responses*)

evaluative/comparison

PART II: ORAL READING AND ANALYSIS OF MISCUES

Directions: Say, "Now I would like to hear you read this story out loud." Have the student read orally until the sample is completed. Follow along on the Miscue Grid, marking any oral reading errors as appropriate. *Remember to count miscues only up to the point in the story containing the oral reading stop-marker (///).* Then complete the Developmental/Performance Summary to determine whether to continue the assessment. (*Note:* The Miscue Grid should be completed *after* the assessment session has been concluded in order to minimize stress for the student.)

ERROR TYPES　　　　ERROR ANALYSIS

Animal Friends	mis-pronun.	sub-stitute	inser-tions	tchr. assist	omis-sions	Error Totals	Self-Correct.	(M) Meaning	(S) Syntax	(V) Visual
There are many kinds of animals.										
Some animals are our friends. Others are not.										
Dogs and cats can be good friends.										
Dogs and cats make sounds to talk to us.										
Some dogs bark when they hear something.										
Some dogs bark when they are hungry.										
Cats purr when they are happy.										
Cats meow when they are hungry.										
Not all cats and dogs are your friends.										
If you do not know a dog, do not pet it.										
It might bite you.										
Cats can hurt you too.										
Cats have claws and they can bite.//										
TOTALS										

Summary of Reading Behaviors (Strengths and Needs)

PART III: MISCUE ANALYSIS

Directions: Circle all reading behaviors you observed.

A. Fundamental Behaviors Observed:

L → R Directionality   1 to 1 Matching   Searching for Clues   Cross-Checking

B. Word Attack Behaviors:

No Attempt   Mispronunciation (Invented word)   Substitutes

Skips/Reads On   Asks for Help   Repeats   Attempts to Self-Correct

"Sounds Out" (Segmenting)   Blends Sounds   Structural Analysis (Root words, Affixes)

C. Cueing Systems Used in Attempting Words

CUEING TOOL	MISCUE EXAMPLES	ACTUAL TEXT
(M) Meaning		
(S) Syntax		
(V) Visual		

D. Fluency (word by word → fluent reading)

Word by Word _____   Mixed Phrasing _____   Fluent Reading _____   Fluency Rate in Seconds _____

Performance Summary

Silent Reading Comprehension

_____ 0–1 questions missed = Easy

_____ 2 questions missed = Adequate

_____ 3+ questions missed = Too hard

Oral Reading Accuracy

_____ 0–1 oral error = Easy

_____ 2–5 oral errors = Adequate

_____ 6+ oral errors = Too hard

Continue to the next reading passage? _____ Yes   _____ No

PART IV: LISTENING COMPREHENSION

Directions: If you have decided not to continue to have the student read any other passages, then use this passage to begin assessing the student's listening comprehension (see page 19). Begin by reading the background statement for this passage and then say, "I am going to read this story to you. Please listen carefully because I will be asking you some questions after I finish reading it to you." After reading the passage, ask the student the questions associated with the passage. If the student correctly answers more than six questions, you will need to move to the next level and repeat the procedure.

Listening Comprehension

_____ 0–2 questions missed = move to the next passage level

_____ more than 2 questions missed = stop assessment or move down a level

Examiner's Notes:

LEVEL 2 ASSESSMENT PROTOCOLS

Making Pictures Is Art (142 words)

PART I: SILENT READING COMPREHENSION

Background Statement: "This story is about how we create art. Read it and try to remember some of the important facts about making pictures because I'm going to ask you to tell me about what you have read."

Teacher Directions: Once the student completes the silent reading, say, "Tell me about the story you just read." Answers to the questions below that the student provides during the retelling should be marked "ua" in the appropriate blank to indicate that this response was unaided. Ask all remaining questions not addressed during the retelling and mark those the student answers with an "a" to indicate that the correct response was given after prompting by the teacher.

Questions/Answers

Level of Comprehension/ Expository Grammar Element

_____ 1. Where around us do we find art?
(*everywhere; or the student may name several places*)

literal/description

_____ 2. All art has several things in common (alike). Can you name two?
(*line, shape, and/or color*)

literal/collection

_____ 3. What is an *artist*?
(*someone who creates art, or a similar response*)

literal/description

_____ 4. Lines can be different. What are two ways lines can be different?
(*thick, thin, short, long*)

literal/comparison

_____ 5. What are the three main colors?
(*red, yellow, blue*)

literal/collection

_____ 6. What can you do to make a brand new color?
(*mix two or more of the main colors*)

inferential/problem-solution

_____ 7. Why are white and black NOT one of the main colors?
(*they don't contain red, yellow, or blue*)

literal/comparison

_____ 8. A person may look at a drawing and say that he thinks it is beautiful art. Another person can look at the very same drawing and say that she thinks it is bad art. Why do people sometimes disagree about what is good or bad art?
(*accept any reasonable response, but something implicit of "art is in the eye of the beholder" is best*)

evaluative/comparison

PART II: ORAL READING AND ANALYSIS OF MISCUES

Directions: Say, "Now I would like to hear you read this story out loud." Have the student read orally until the 100-word sample is completed. Follow along on the Miscue Grid, marking any oral reading errors as appropriate. *Remember to count miscues only up to the point in the story containing the oral reading stop-marker (//).* Then complete the Developmental/Performance Summary to determine whether to continue the assessment. (*Note:* The Miscue Grid should be completed *after* the assessment session has been concluded in order to minimize stress for the student.)

ERROR TYPES | | | | | | ERROR ANALYSIS

Making Pictures Is Art

	mis-pronun.	sub-stitute	inser-tions	tchr. assist	omis-sions	Error Totals	Self-Correct.	(M) Meaning	(S) Syntax	(V) Visual
Look around and you can see art everywhere.										
Look at things in your bedroom. They all										
have lines, shape, and color. People who do										
art, or *artists*, use lines, shape, and color to										
make pictures. Lines can be thick or thin.										
Lines can be short or long. You would need to										
use lines to draw your face. Lines are used to										
make shapes. In your room at home, your										
bed, night light, and wall have shape. These										
things also have color. Red, yellow, and blue										
are the main colors. All other colors can be										
made by mixing these colors. Orange//*is*										
made by mixing red and yellow.										
TOTALS										

Summary of Reading Behaviors (Strengths and Needs)

PART III: MISCUE ANALYSIS

Directions: *Circle all reading behaviors you observed.*

A. Fundamental Behaviors Observed:

L → R Directionality   1 to 1 Matching   Searching for Clues   Cross-Checking

B. Word Attack Behaviors:

No Attempt   Mispronunciation (Invented word)   Substitutes

Skips/Reads On   Asks for Help   Repeats   Attempts to Self-Correct

"Sounds Out" (Segmenting)   Blends Sounds   Structural Analysis (Root words, Affixes)

C. Cueing Systems Used in Attempting Words

CUEING TOOL	MISCUE EXAMPLES	ACTUAL TEXT
(M) Meaning		
(S) Syntax		
(V) Visual		

D. Fluency (word by word → fluent reading)

Word by Word _____   Mixed Phrasing _____   Fluent Reading _____   Fluency Rate in Seconds _____

Performance Summary

Silent Reading Comprehension

_____ 0–1 questions missed = Easy

_____ 2 questions missed = Adequate

_____ 3+ questions missed = Too hard

Oral Reading Accuracy

_____ 0–1 oral error = Easy

_____ 2–5 oral errors = Adequate

_____ 6+ oral errors = Too hard

Continue to the next reading passage? _____ Yes   _____ No

PART IV: LISTENING COMPREHENSION

Directions: If you have decided not to continue to have the student read any other passages, then use this passage to begin assessing the student's listening comprehension (see page 19). Begin by reading the background statement for this passage and then say, "I am going to read this story to you. Please listen carefully because I will be asking you some questions after I finish reading it to you." After reading the passage, ask the student the questions associated with the passage. If the student correctly answers more than six questions, you will need to move to the next level and repeat the procedure.

Listening Comprehension

_____ 0–2 questions missed = move to the next passage level

_____ more than 2 questions missed = stop assessment or move down a level

Examiner's Notes:

LEVEL 3 ASSESSMENT PROTOCOLS

The History of Books (186 words)

PART I: SILENT READING COMPREHENSION

Background Statement: "This story is about how books were first made. Read it and try to remember some of the important facts about books because I'm going to ask you to tell me about what you have read."

Teacher Directions: Once the student completes the silent reading, say, "Tell me about the story you just read." Answers to the questions below that the student provides during the retelling should be marked "ua" in the appropriate blank to indicate that this response was unaided. Ask all remaining questions not addressed during the retelling and mark those the student answers with an "a" to indicate that the correct response was given after prompting by the teacher.

Questions/Answers

Level of Comprehension/ Expository Grammar Element

_____ 1. Why were there so few books a long time ago?
  (*the printing press hadn't been invented*)

literal/causation

_____ 2. How were early books produced?
  (*they were hand written on skin or paper*)

inferential/problem-solution

_____ 3. Early books were written on what kinds of skin?
  (*sheep and calf*)

literal/description

_____ 4. Why were animal skins preferred to paper when making a book a long time ago?
  (*animal skins were stronger than paper*)

literal/comparison

_____ 5. Early in the history of books only the rich had books. Why?
  (*because the cost of making the books made them expensive*)

inferential/causation

_____ 6. What invention allowed people who were not rich to begin reading books?
  (*printing press*)

literal/problem-solution

_____ 7. Why could it have taken a whole flock of sheep to make a book?
  (*because it took one sheepskin for each page*)

literal/causation

_____ 8. How has the invention of the printing press helped people throughout the world?
  (*response should be related to the ideas of more people learned to read, people can learn about lots of different topics, or other plausible responses*)

evaluative/comparison

PART II: ORAL READING AND ANALYSIS OF MISCUES

Directions: Say, "Now I would like to hear you read this story out loud." Have the student read orally until the 100-word sample is completed. Follow along on the Miscue Grid, marking any oral reading errors as appropriate. *Remember to count miscues only up to the point in the story containing the oral reading stop-marker (//).* Then complete the Developmental/Performance Summary to determine whether to continue the assessment. (*Note:* The Miscue Grid should be completed *after* the assessment session has been concluded in order to minimize stress for the student.)

ERROR ANALYSIS

ERROR TYPES

The History of Books	mis-pronun.	sub-stitute	inser-tions	tchr. assist	omis-sions	Error Totals	Self-Correct.	(M) Meaning	(S) Syntax	(V) Visual
The history of books is interesting. A long										
time ago most people could not read. The										
people who could read didn't have many										
books to read. They didn't have many books										
because the printing press had not been										
invented. All books had to be hand written										
on either an animal skin or a kind of paper.										
Most books were written on stretched										
sheepskin or stretched calfskin. The cost										
of writing a book on skin limited how										
many could be made. Only the rich										
could own books. Most books were written										
on skins because they were stronger and										
prettier than those// *written on paper.*										
TOTALS										

Summary of Reading Behaviors (Strengths and Needs)

PART III: MISCUE ANALYSIS

Directions: Circle all reading behaviors you observed.

A. Fundamental Behaviors Observed:

L → R Directionality   1 to 1 Matching   Searching for Clues   Cross-Checking

B. Word Attack Behaviors:

No Attempt   Mispronunciation (Invented word)   Substitutes

Skips/Reads On   Asks for Help   Repeats   Attempts to Self-Correct

"Sounds Out" (Segmenting)   Blends Sounds   Structural Analysis (Root words, Affixes)

C. Cueing Systems Used in Attempting Words

CUEING TOOL	MISCUE EXAMPLES	ACTUAL TEXT
(M) Meaning		
(S) Syntax		
(V) Visual		

D. Fluency (word by word → fluent reading)

Word by Word _____   Mixed Phrasing _____   Fluent Reading _____   Fluency Rate in Seconds _____

Performance Summary

Silent Reading Comprehension

_____ 0–1 questions missed = Easy

_____ 2 questions missed = Adequate

_____ 3+ questions missed = Too hard

Oral Reading Accuracy

_____ 0–1 oral error = Easy

_____ 2–5 oral errors = Adequate

_____ 6+ oral errors = Too hard

Continue to the next reading passage? _____ Yes   _____ No

PART IV: LISTENING COMPREHENSION

Directions: If you have decided not to continue to have the student read any other passages, then use this passage to begin assessing the student's listening comprehension (see page 19). Begin by reading the background statement for this passage and then say, "I am going to read this story to you. Please listen carefully because I will be asking you some questions after I finish reading it to you." After reading the passage, ask the student the questions associated with the passage. If the student correctly answers more than six questions, you will need to move to the next level and repeat the procedure.

Listening Comprehension

_____ 0–2 questions missed = move to the next passage level

_____ more than 2 questions missed = stop assessment or move down a level

Examiner's Notes:

LEVEL 4 ASSESSMENT PROTOCOLS

Mountain Man (249 words)

PART I: SILENT READING COMPREHENSION

Background Statement: "This story is about a man who went to live in the mountains. Read it and try to remember some of the important facts about this mountain man because I'm going to ask you to tell me about what you have read."

Teacher Directions: Once the student completes the silent reading, say, "Tell me about the story you just read." Answers to the questions below that the student provides during the retelling should be marked "ua" in the appropriate blank to indicate that this response was unaided. Ask all remaining questions not addressed during the retelling and mark those the student answers with an "a" to indicate that the correct response was given after prompting by the teacher.

Questions/Answers

Level of Comprehension/ Expository Grammar Element

_____ 1. Who was the famous mountain man the story was about?
(*Jim Beckwourth*)

literal/description

_____ 2. What four things did most mountain men take with them into the mountains?
(*gun, knife, coffee, flour*)

literal/collection

_____ 3. What made Jim Beckwourth go to the mountains?
(*he wanted to escape slavery*)

literal/causation

_____ 4. What animal did Jim trap?
(*beaver*)

inferential/causation

_____ 5. Why would mountain men want to be on good terms with the Indians?
(*accept plausible responses*)

evaluative/problem-solution

_____ 6. What did the author mean by "he discovered a pass through the mountains"?
(*he meant he found a way to get through the mountains that was easier than other ways*)

inferential/problem-solution

_____ 7. What kind of Indian chief did Jim become?
(*Crow*)

literal/causation

_____ 8. Who did Jim marry?
(*an Indian squaw*)

literal/causation

PART II: ORAL READING AND ANALYSIS OF MISCUES

Directions: Say, "Now I would like to hear you read this story out loud." Have the student read orally until the 100-word sample is completed. Follow along on the Miscue Grid, marking any oral reading errors as appropriate. *Remember to count miscues only up to the point in the story containing the oral reading stop-marker (///).* Then complete the Developmental/Performance Summary to determine whether to continue the assessment. (*Note:* The Miscue Grid should be completed *after* the assessment session has been concluded in order to minimize stress for the student.)

ERROR TYPES / ERROR ANALYSIS

Mountain Man	mis-pronun.	sub-stitute	inser-tions	tchr. assist	omis-sions	Error Totals	Self-Correct.	(M) Meaning	(S) Syntax	(V) Visual
During the early history of our country,										
the West was full of stories about cowboys										
and Indians. Another group that helped settle										
the West were the mountain men. These were										
men who wanted to trap animals for their furs.										
These men went into unknown parts of the										
West beyond the Rocky Mountains. They										
carried a gun, a knife, coffee, flour, and little										
else. They planned to eat the animals they										
shot and the berries they found. They went to										
trap beaver for their furs. Some of these men										
made friends with the Indians who										
lived in the far West. Others// did not.										
TOTALS										

Summary of Reading Behaviors (Strengths and Needs)

PART III: MISCUE ANALYSIS

Directions: *Circle all reading behaviors you observed.*

A. Fundamental Behaviors Observed:

L → R Directionality   1 to 1 Matching   Searching for Clues   Cross-Checking

B. Word Attack Behaviors:

No Attempt   Mispronunciation (Invented word)   Substitutes

Skips/Reads On   Asks for Help   Repeats   Attempts to Self-Correct

"Sounds Out" (Segmenting)   Blends Sounds   Structural Analysis (Root words, Affixes)

C. Cueing Systems Used In Attempting Words

CUEING TOOL	MISCUE EXAMPLES	ACTUAL TEXT
(M) Meaning		
(S) Syntax		
(V) Visual		

D. Fluency (word by word → fluent reading)

Word by Word _____   Mixed Phrasing _____   Fluent Reading _____   Fluency Rate in Seconds _____

Performance Summary

Silent Reading Comprehension

_____ 0–1 questions missed = Easy

_____ 2 questions missed = Adequate

_____ 3+ questions missed = Too hard

Oral Reading Accuracy

_____ 0–1 oral error = Easy

_____ 2–5 oral errors = Adequate

_____ 6+ oral errors = Too hard

Continue to the next reading passage? _____ Yes   _____ No

PART IV: LISTENING COMPREHENSION

Directions: If you have decided not to continue to have the student read any other passages, then use this passage to begin assessing the student's listening comprehension (see page 19). Begin by reading the background statement for this passage and then say, "I am going to read this story to you. Please listen carefully because I will be asking you some questions after I finish reading it to you." After reading the passage, ask the student the questions associated with the passage. If the student correctly answers more than six questions, you will need to move to the next level and repeat the procedure.

Listening Comprehension

_____ 0–2 questions missed = move to the next passage level

_____ more than 2 questions missed = stop assessment or move down a level

Examiner's Notes:

LEVEL 5 ASSESSMENT PROTOCOLS

Music of Mexico (274 words)

PART I: SILENT READING COMPREHENSION

Background Statement: "This story is about music that people in Mexico enjoy. Read it and try to remember some of the important facts about their music because I'm going to ask you to tell me about what you have read."

Teacher Directions: Once the student completes the silent reading, say, "Tell me about the story you just read." Answers to the questions below that the student provides during the retelling should be marked "ua" in the appropriate blank to indicate that this response was unaided. Ask all remaining questions not addressed during the retelling and mark those the student answers with an "a" to indicate that the correct response was given after prompting by the teacher.

Questions/Answers

Level of Comprehension/ Expository Grammar Element

_____ 1. Where is Mexico located?
(*south of the United States*)

literal/description

_____ 2. What types of events are celebrated with music in Mexico?
(*weddings, birthdays, anniversaries*)

literal/collection

_____ 3. Musical groups from the eastern part of Mexico differ from those in the west. Can you name two instruments used in western Mexico that musicians in eastern Mexico don't use?
(*violins and trumpets*)

inferential/comparison

_____ 4. What is the name of a famous song from the eastern part of Mexico?
(*La Bamba*)

literal/collection

_____ 5. What does the word *mariachi* refer to in the passage you just read?
(*a musical group from the western part of Mexico*)

literal/vocabulary

_____ 6. How do Mexicans show that they enjoy music?
(*they sing along, dance, laugh, and clap*)

inferential/comparison

_____ 7. How many instruments are used by bands from the eastern part of Mexico?
(*four*)

literal/collection

_____ 8. Many people who come to the United States from other countries adapt to the lifestyle here. They do not give up the music of their homeland. Why?
(*accept plausible responses associated with the importance of music keeping them in touch with their culture*)

evaluative/comparison

PART II: ORAL READING AND ANALYSIS OF MISCUES

Directions: Say, "Now I would like to hear you read this story out loud." Have the student read orally until the 100-word sample is completed. Follow along on the Miscue Grid, marking any oral reading errors as appropriate. *Remember to count miscues only up to the point in the story containing the oral reading stop-marker (//).* Then complete the Developmental/Performance Summary to determine whether to continue the assessment. (*Note:* The Miscue Grid should be completed *after* the assessment session has been concluded in order to minimize stress for the student.)

	ERROR TYPES							ERROR ANALYSIS		
	mis-pronun.	sub-stitute	inser-tions	tchr. assist	omis-sions	Error Totals	Self-Correct.	(M) Meaning	(S) Syntax	(V) Visual
Music of Mexico										
Much of the music you hear in the United										
States comes from other countries. Most										
people who come to the United States from										
other countries adapt to the lifestyle here.										
However, they do not give up the music										
of their homelands. Many people have										
come to the United States from Mexico.										
Mexico is a large country that lies										
south of the United States. The music of										
Mexico is unique and has contributed										
much to the music heard in the United										
States. Music from Mexico often uses										
instruments such as the folk harp, violin,										
and various types of guitars. Music in //										
Mexico is used to celebrate birthdays,										
weddings, anniversaries, and other holidays.										
TOTALS										

Summary of Reading Behaviors (Strengths and Needs)

PART III: MISCUE ANALYSIS

Directions: *Circle all reading behaviors you observed.*

A. Fundamental Behaviors Observed:

L → R Directionality   1 to 1 Matching   Searching for Clues   Cross-Checking

B. Word Attack Behaviors:

No Attempt   Mispronunciation (Invented word)   Substitutes

Skips/Reads On   Asks for Help   Repeats   Attempts to Self-Correct

"Sounds Out" (Segmenting)   Blends Sounds   Structural Analysis (Root words, Affixes)

C. Cueing Systems Used in Attempting Words

CUEING TOOL	MISCUE EXAMPLES	ACTUAL TEXT
(M) Meaning		
(S) Syntax		
(V) Visual		

D. Fluency (word by word → fluent reading)

Word by Word _____   Mixed Phrasing _____   Fluent Reading _____   Fluency Rate in Seconds _____

Performance Summary

Silent Reading Comprehension

_____ 0–1 questions missed = Easy

_____ 2 questions missed = Adequate

_____ 3+ questions missed = Too hard

Oral Reading Accuracy

_____ 0–1 oral error = Easy

_____ 2–5 oral errors = Adequate

_____ 6+ oral errors = Too hard

Continue to the next reading passage? _____ Yes   _____ No

PART IV: LISTENING COMPREHENSION

Directions: If you have decided not to continue to have the student read any other passages, then use this passage to begin assessing the student's listening comprehension (see page 19). Begin by reading the background statement for this passage and then say, "I am going to read this story to you. Please listen carefully because I will be asking you some questions after I finish reading it to you." After reading the passage, ask the student the questions associated with the passage. If the student correctly answers more than six questions, you will need to move to the next level and repeat the procedure.

Listening Comprehension

_____ 0–2 questions missed = move to the next passage level

_____ more than 2 questions missed = stop assessment or move down a level

Examiner's Notes:

LEVEL 6 ASSESSMENT PROTOCOLS

Jesse Owens (277 words)

PART I: SILENT READING COMPREHENSION

Background Statement: "This story is about a famous athlete in the 1936 Olympics. Read it and try to remember some of the important facts about this man because I'm going to ask you to tell me about what you have read."

Teacher Directions: Once the student completes the silent reading, say, "Tell me about the story you just read." Answers to the questions below that the student provides during the retelling should be marked "ua" in the appropriate blank to indicate that this response was unaided. Ask all remaining questions not addressed during the retelling and mark those the student answers with an "a" to indicate that the correct response was given after prompting by the teacher.

Questions/Answers

	Level of Comprehension/ Expository Grammar Element

_____ 1. Where were the 1936 Olympic Games held?
(*Germany*)

literal/collection

_____ 2. Who ruled Germany during this time?
(*Adolf Hitler*)

literal/collection

_____ 3. Why did some Americans think we should not send
a team and stay home?
(*Hitler had been mistreating German Jews, or
German racism*)

literal/problem-solution

_____ 4. Why did black athletes at the time question whether
they should go to the Olympics?
(*American racism*)

literal/comparison

_____ 5. What did Jesse Owens do during the 1936 Olympics?
(*led the U.S. team to victory and/or won 4 Gold Medals*)

literal/collection

_____ 6. How did Jesse Owens's accomplishments help the U.S.?
(*they helped move the U.S. toward equal treatment for
all Americans*)

literal/causation

_____ 7. How was Adolf Hitler like slave owners during the
early part of the United States's history?
(*he thought he had the right to own people*)

inferential/comparison

_____ 8. In our story we read about how Jesse Owens fought
racism. What does it mean to say someone is a *racist*?
(*accept plausible responses but they should relate to the
idea of mistreating another person or thinking your
own race is superior to others*)

evaluative/comparison

PART II: ORAL READING AND ANALYSIS OF MISCUES

Directions: Say, "Now I would like to hear you read this story out loud." Have the student read orally until the 100-word sample is completed. Follow along on the Miscue Grid, marking any oral reading errors as appropriate. *Remember to count miscues only up to the point in the story containing the oral reading stop-marker (///).* Then complete the Developmental/Performance Summary to determine whether to continue the assessment. (*Note:* The Miscue Grid should be completed *after* the assessment session has been concluded in order to minimize stress for the student.)

ERROR TYPES | | | | | | | ERROR ANALYSIS

	mis-pronun.	sub-stitute	inser-tions	tchr. assist	omis-sions	Error Totals	Self-Correct.	(M) Meaning	(S) Syntax	(V) Visual
Jesse Owens										
In 1936, the Olympic games were to										
be held in Germany. For months before										
the games took place, a stormy argument										
took place in the United States. Germany										
was ruled by Adolf Hitler and the Nazi Party.										
Hitler had been mistreating German Jews for										
some time, and many people in the United										
States wondered whether we should send										
a team or stay home and protest German										
racism. It was finally decided that we should										
send a team. At the same time, many black										
athletes wondered if they should go because										
of racism in the United States. Finally, led										
by Jesse // Owens, the black American athletes										
decided they should go to Germany to										
show the Germans how great they were.										
TOTALS										

Summary of Reading Behaviors (Strengths and Needs)

PART III: MISCUE ANALYSIS

Directions: *Circle all reading behaviors you observed.*

A. Fundamental Behaviors Observed:

L → R Directionality   1 to 1 Matching   Searching for Clues   Cross-Checking

B. Word Attack Behaviors:

No Attempt   Mispronunciation (Invented word)   Substitutes

Skips/Reads On   Asks for Help   Repeats   Attempts to Self-Correct

"Sounds Out" (Segmenting)   Blends Sounds   Structural Analysis (Root words, Affixes)

C. Cueing Systems Used in Attempting Words

CUEING TOOL	MISCUE EXAMPLES	ACTUAL TEXT
(M) Meaning		
(S) Syntax		
(V) Visual		

D. Fluency (word by word → fluent reading)

Word by Word _____   Mixed Phrasing _____   Fluent Reading _____   Fluency Rate in Seconds _____

Performance Summary

Silent Reading Comprehension

_____ 0–1 questions missed = Easy

_____ 2 questions missed = Adequate

_____ 3+ questions missed = Too hard

Oral Reading Accuracy

_____ 0–1 oral error = Easy

_____ 2–5 oral errors = Adequate

_____ 6+ oral errors = Too hard

Continue to the next reading passage? _____ Yes   _____ No

PART IV: LISTENING COMPREHENSION

Directions: If you have decided not to continue to have the student read any other passages, then use this passage to begin assessing the student's listening comprehension (see page 19). Begin by reading the background statement for this passage and then say, "I am going to read this story to you. Please listen carefully because I will be asking you some questions after I finish reading it to you." After reading the passage, ask the student the questions associated with the passage. If the student correctly answers more than six questions, you will need to move to the next level and repeat the procedure.

Listening Comprehension

_____ 0–2 questions missed = move to the next passage level

_____ more than 2 questions missed = stop assessment or move down a level

Examiner's Notes:

LEVEL 7 ASSESSMENT PROTOCOLS

Nails: A Carpenter's "Fastener" (410 words)

PART I: SILENT READING COMPREHENSION

Background Statement: "This story is about the different kinds of nails used by carpenters. Read it and try to remember some of the important facts about nails because I'm going to ask you to tell me about what you have read."

Teacher Directions: Once the student completes the silent reading, say, "Tell me about the story you just read." Answers to the questions below that the student provides during the retelling should be marked "ua" in the appropriate blank to indicate that this response was unaided. Ask all remaining questions not addressed during the retelling and mark those the student answers with an "a" to indicate that the correct response was given after prompting by the teacher.

Questions/Answers

*Level of Comprehension/
Expository Grammar Element*

_____ 1. Other than nails, what are two widely used fasteners?
(*screws and bolts*)

literal/collection

_____ 2. What is the most common explanation of how the penny system originated?
(*most people think the penny system originated by the weight of 100 nails determining the price*)

inferential/causation

_____ 3. What are the three common types of wire nails?
(*common, box, finish*)

literal/collection

_____ 4. What is the difference between wire nails and cut nails?
(*cut nails are stamped from metal sheets while wire nails are cut from rolls of wire*)

inferential/comparison

_____ 5. What does the term "gauge" mean in reference to nails?
(*thickness*)

literal/vocabulary

_____ 6. What is a difference between common nails and finish nails?
(*common nails are thicker and have a larger head than finish nails*)

inferential/comparison

_____ 7. Why are finish nails preferred for fastening edges of wood?
(*they are thin and are less likely to cause the wood to split*)

inferential/comparison

_____ 8. What is the motto of many carpenters?
(*always use the right tool for the right job*)

literal/collection

PART II: ORAL READING AND ANALYSIS OF MISCUES

Directions: Say, "Now I would like to hear you read this story out loud." Have the student read orally until the 100-word sample is completed. Follow along on the Miscue Grid, marking any oral reading errors as appropriate. *Remember to count miscues only up to the point in the story containing the oral reading stop-marker (///).* Then complete the Developmental/Performance Summary to determine whether to continue the assessment. (*Note:* The Miscue Grid should be completed *after* the assessment session has been concluded in order to minimize stress for the student.)

	mis-pronun.	sub-stitute	inser-tions	tchr. assist	omis-sions	Error Totals	Self-Correct.	(M) Meaning	(S) Syntax	(V) Visual
Nails: A Carpenter's "Fastener"										
Carpenters use a variety of tools in their										
profession such as hammers, saws, and power										
tools. They also use what are called *fasteners*										
to hold pieces of wood and other materials										
together. The most widely used fasteners are										
nails, screws, and bolts. Nails are perhaps the										
most commonly used fasteners in the										
carpenter's toolbox. There are literally										
hundreds of kinds of nails that can be used										
for just about any kind of fastening job. The										
size of nails is usually designated using the										
penny system. While we are not exactly sure										
how the penny system came about, many										
people believe// *that it is an ancient*										
measurement based on the price of nails										
according to weight per one hundred nails.										
TOTALS										

Summary of Reading Behaviors (Strengths and Needs)

PART III: MISCUE ANALYSIS

Directions: Circle all reading behaviors you observed.

A. Fundamental Behaviors Observed:

L → R Directionality   1 to 1 Matching   Searching for Clues   Cross-Checking

B. Word Attack Behaviors:

No Attempt   Mispronunciation (Invented word)   Substitutes

Skips/Reads On   Asks for Help   Repeats   Attempts to Self-Correct

"Sounds Out" (Segmenting)   Blends Sounds   Structural Analysis (Root words, Affixes)

C. Cueing Systems Used In Attempting Words

CUEING TOOL	MISCUE EXAMPLES	ACTUAL TEXT
(M) Meaning		
(S) Syntax		
(V) Visual		

D. Fluency (word by word → fluent reading)

Word by Word _____   Mixed Phrasing _____   Fluent Reading _____   Fluency Rate in Seconds _____

Performance Summary

Silent Reading Comprehension

_____ 0–1 questions missed = Easy

_____ 2 questions missed = Adequate

_____ 3+ questions missed = Too hard

Oral Reading Accuracy

_____ 0–1 oral error = Easy

_____ 2–5 oral errors = Adequate

_____ 6+ oral errors = Too hard

Continue to the next reading passage? _____ Yes   _____ No

PART IV: LISTENING COMPREHENSION

Directions: If you have decided not to continue to have the student read any other passages, then use this passage to begin assessing the student's listening comprehension (see page 19). Begin by reading the background statement for this passage and then say, "I am going to read this story to you. Please listen carefully because I will be asking you some questions after I finish reading it to you." After reading the passage, ask the student the questions associated with the passage. If the student correctly answers more than six questions, you will need to move to the next level and repeat the procedure.

Listening Comprehension

_____ 0–2 questions missed = move to the next passage level

_____ more than 2 questions missed = stop assessment or move down a level

Examiner's Notes:

D LEVEL 8 ASSESSMENT PROTOCOLS

The Environments of Africa (510 words)

PART I: SILENT READING COMPREHENSION

Background Statement: "This story is about parts of Africa. Read it and try to remember some of the important facts about this continent because I'm going to ask you to tell me about what you have read."

Teacher Directions: Once the student completes the silent reading, say, "Tell me about the story you just read." Answers to the questions below that the student provides during the retelling should be marked "ua" in the appropriate blank to indicate that this response was unaided. Ask all remaining questions not addressed during the retelling and mark those the student answers with an "a" to indicate that the correct response was given after prompting by the teacher.

Questions/Answers

Level of Comprehension/ Expository Grammar Element

_____ 1. What four bodies of water nearly surround Africa?
(*Atlantic and Indian Oceans, Mediterranean and Red Seas*)

literal/collection

_____ 2. Why are the countries in Central and West Africa thinly populated?
(*lack of suitable soil for farming*)

literal/causation

_____ 3. Which section of Africa is often called the sub-Sahara?
(*southern*)

literal/collection

_____ 4. What are *savannas*?
(*grasslands*)

literal/vocabulary

_____ 5. In which part of Africa is the Sahara Desert located?
(*northern*)

literal/description

_____ 6. What type of political change occurred in South Africa during the latter portion of the 20th century?
(*South Africa became a democracy because everyone was given the right to vote*)

literal/causation

_____ 7. What is the name of the region of Africa where the countries of Ethiopia and Somalia are located?
(*African Horn*)

literal/collection

_____ 8. What causes the climate of the sub-Sahara to be warm and moist?
(*the equator runs through the sub-Sahara*)

literal/causation

PART II: ORAL READING AND ANALYSIS OF MISCUES

Directions: Say, "Now I would like to hear you read this story out loud." Have the student read orally until the 100-word sample is completed. Follow along on the Miscue Grid, marking any oral reading errors as appropriate. *Remember to count miscues only up to the point in the story containing the oral reading stop-marker (///).* Then complete the Developmental/Performance Summary to determine whether to continue the assessment. (*Note:* The Miscue Grid should be completed *after* the assessment session has been concluded in order to minimize stress for the student.)

	mis-pronun.	sub-stitute	inser-tions	tchr. assist	omis-sions	Error Totals	Self-Correct.	(M) Meaning	(S) Syntax	(V) Visual
The Environments of Africa										
Africa is the Earth's second largest continent.										
It is home to about one-tenth of the world										
population. While it is about three times										
larger than the United States in terms of										
landmass, many people still do not know										
very much about it. Some think of Africa										
as a single country and it is not. In this										
selection we take a brief tour of this continent.										
Africa is almost completely surrounded by										
water. Two oceans and two seas are on her										
borders. The Atlantic Ocean borders Africa										
on the east, while the Indian Ocean borders										
to the west. The Mediterranean Sea //										
and the Red Sea are to the north.										
TOTALS										

Summary of Reading Behaviors (Strengths and Needs)

PART III: MISCUE ANALYSIS

Directions: Circle all reading behaviors you observed.

A. Fundamental Behaviors Observed:

L → R Directionality   1 to 1 Matching   Searching for Clues   Cross-Checking

B. Word Attack Behaviors:

No Attempt   Mispronunciation (Invented word)   Substitutes

Skips/Reads On   Asks for Help   Repeats   Attempts to Self-Correct

"Sounds Out" (Segmenting)   Blends Sounds   Structural Analysis (Root words, Affixes)

C. Cueing Systems Used in Attempting Words

CUEING TOOL	MISCUE EXAMPLES	ACTUAL TEXT
(M) Meaning		
(S) Syntax		
(V) Visual		

D. Fluency (word by word → fluent reading)

Word by Word _____   Mixed Phrasing _____   Fluent Reading _____   Fluency Rate in Seconds _____

Performance Summary

Silent Reading Comprehension

_____ 0–1 questions missed = Easy

_____ 2 questions missed = Adequate

_____ 3+ questions missed = Too hard

Oral Reading Accuracy

_____ 0–1 oral error = Easy

_____ 2–5 oral errors = Adequate

_____ 6+ oral errors = Too hard

Continue to the next reading passage? _____ Yes   _____ No

PART IV: LISTENING COMPREHENSION

Directions: If you have decided not to continue to have the student read any other passages, then use this passage to begin assessing the student's listening comprehension (see page 19). Begin by reading the background statement for this passage and then say, "I am going to read this story to you. Please listen carefully because I will be asking you some questions after I finish reading it to you." After reading the passage, ask the student the questions associated with the passage. If the student correctly answers more than six questions, you will need to move to the next level and repeat the procedure.

Listening Comprehension

_____ 0–2 questions missed = move to the next passage level

_____ more than 2 questions missed = stop assessment or move down a level

Examiner's Notes:

LEVEL 9 ASSESSMENT PROTOCOLS

The Mathematics of Health (249 words)

PART I: SILENT READING COMPREHENSION

Background Statement: "This story is about the foods we eat. Read it and try to remember some of the important facts because I'm going to ask you to tell me about what you have read."

Teacher Directions: Once the student completes the silent reading, say, "Tell me about the story you just read." Answers to the questions below that the student provides during the retelling should be marked "ua" in the appropriate blank to indicate that this response was unaided. Ask all remaining questions not addressed during the retelling and mark those the student answers with an "a" to indicate that the correct response was given after prompting by the teacher.

Questions/Answers

*Level of Comprehension/
Expository Grammar Element*

_____ 1. What has caused more and more people to try and stay healthy?
(*rising cost of health care*)

inferential/causation

_____ 2. What were the four things people try to limit the amount of in their diets?
(*sugar, fat, salt/sodium, cholesterol*)

literal/collection

_____ 3. What was an initial problem with products labeled Lo-Cal or LITE?
(*they weren't really any healthier than foods that didn't have the labels*)

literal/problem-solution

_____ 4. According to the passage, how can comparing food labels benefit the health-conscious buyer?
(*a person can select foods that have less fat content or less caloric content*)

inferential/problem-solution

_____ 5. What caused companies to begin providing nutritional information on their products?
(*Food and Drug Administration rules*)

literal/causation

_____ 6. The title of this selection is "The Mathematics of Health." Why is this an appropriate title?
(*accept plausible responses related to the idea of determining the amounts of fat, salt, etc., in food*)

inferential/problem-solution

_____ 7. What did the selection indicate as the optimum amount of calories per day for a grown person?
(*1500*)

literal/collection

_____ 8. What does the lower case "g" mean on a food label that says a food has 20g of fat?
(*grams*)

literal/description

PART II: ORAL READING AND ANALYSIS OF MISCUES

Directions: Say, "Now I would like to hear you read this story out loud." Have the student read orally until the 100-word sample is completed. Follow along on the Miscue Grid, marking any oral reading errors as appropriate. *Remember to count miscues only up to the point in the story containing the oral reading stop-marker (///).* Then complete the Developmental/Performance Summary to determine whether to continue the assessment. (*Note:* The Miscue Grid should be completed *after* the assessment session has been concluded in order to minimize stress for the student.)

ERROR TYPES / ERROR ANALYSIS

	mis-pronun.	sub-stitute	inser-tions	tchr. assist	omis-sions	Error Totals	Self-Correct.	(M) Meaning	(S) Syntax	(V) Visual
The Mathematics of Health										
Americans spend billions of dollars every										
year on medical care. Doctor bills, medicine,										
dental work, optical products (glasses,										
contacts, etc.), health insurance, nursing										
homes, and other health-related costs are all										
part of the health care picture. As the										
associated costs of medical care continue										
to escalate, more and more Americans are										
making efforts to stay healthy in a myriad of										
ways. These efforts range on a continuum										
from daily exercise to careful control of one's										
diet. This passage will focus on the										
mathematics involved in monitoring one's diet.										
People sometimes try to remain healthy by										
limiting the amount of fat, // sodium (salt),										
cholesterol, and sugar in their diet.										
TOTALS										

Summary of Reading Behaviors (Strengths and Needs)

PART III: MISCUE ANALYSIS

Directions: *Circle all reading behaviors you observed.*

A. Fundamental Behaviors Observed:

L → R Directionality   1 to 1 Matching   Searching for Clues   Cross-Checking

B. Word Attack Behaviors:

No Attempt   Mispronunciation (Invented word)   Substitutes

Skips/Reads On   Asks for Help   Repeats   Attempts to Self-Correct

"Sounds Out" (Segmenting)   Blends Sounds   Structural Analysis (Root words, Affixes)

C. Cueing Systems Used in Attempting Words

CUEING TOOL	MISCUE EXAMPLES	ACTUAL TEXT
(M) Meaning		
(S) Syntax		
(V) Visual		

D. Fluency (word by word → fluent reading)

Word by Word _____   Mixed Phrasing _____   Fluent Reading _____   Fluency Rate in Seconds _____

Performance Summary

Silent Reading Comprehension

_____ 0–1 questions missed = Easy

_____ 2 questions missed = Adequate

_____ 3+ questions missed = Too hard

Oral Reading Accuracy

_____ 0–1 oral error = Easy

_____ 2–5 oral errors = Adequate

_____ 6+ oral errors = Too hard

Continue to the next reading passage? _____ Yes   _____ No

PART IV: LISTENING COMPREHENSION

Directions: If you have decided not to continue to have the student read any other passages, then use this passage to begin assessing the student's listening comprehension (see page 19). Begin by reading the background statement for this passage and then say, "I am going to read this story to you. Please listen carefully because I will be asking you some questions after I finish reading it to you." After reading the passage, ask the student the questions associated with the passage. If the student correctly answers more than six questions, you will need to move to the next level and repeat the procedure.

Listening Comprehension

_____ 0–2 questions missed = move to the next passage level

_____ more than 2 questions missed = stop assessment or move down a level

Examiner's Notes:

EXPOSITORY PASSAGES
LEVELS 10–12

Stereo Speakers

Almost everyone has listened to music at one time or another, yet few understand how stereo loudspeakers work. Simply put, all stereo loudspeakers are transducers that change electrical signals from an amplifier into sound waves. Beyond this simplistic explanation, stereo speakers diverge into many different types that even the most enthusiastic music lover can find perplexing. In general, all speakers can be placed into one of two major categories, depending on how the electrical signal is converted to sound.

The most prevalent type of speaker uses *dynamic drivers,* those familiar cones and domes found in both low-cost and expensive models. Basically, this type of speaker has air-exciting diaphragms (cones and domes) that are driven by an electromagnetic component made up of a voice coil and magnet. As an electrical signal is sent from the amplifier, the component moves back and forth. The cone or dome fixed to the voice coil moves with it, resulting in sound waves in the air in front and behind.

The other type of speaker, which produces sound differently from dynamic speakers, is often referred to as a *planar-designed speaker.* This type of speaker, which generally costs substantially more than the dynamic driver type, abandons the use of the voice coil and magnet component in lieu of a flat surface or a long ribbon-like strip that is directly driven by the audio signal from the amplifier to create sound waves. Since most people rarely encounter this type of speaker, the remainder of this discussion will focus on the two major types of dynamic driver speaker.

All dynamic speakers need an enclosure to help prevent something called back wave cancellation. Since all dynamic drivers radiate sound behind as well as in front, if there is no way to control the back wave, it will literally cancel out the front wave, resulting in little or no sound. Thus, the enclosure of a stereo speaker serves to deal with this sonic problem.

The most common type of speaker is the acoustic suspension, or sealed box, speaker, which was developed in the 1950s. In this type of speaker, the woofer (dome) is mounted in an airtight enclosure so that its forward surface radiates freely into the room, while its back wave is lost in the internal volume of the sealed box. Since the back wave cannot radiate out into the room, there is no risk of front wave cancellation and it is possible to get powerful bass from a rather diminutive box. The one limitation of this design is that half its acoustical potential (back wave) is lost. Therefore, an acoustic suspension speaker requires more amplifier power than an equivalent unsealed box to achieve a given level of sound.

The other major type of dynamic speaker is called the bass reflex design. This design uses an enclosure that has a carefully designed opening, or vent, which allows the woofer's back wave to escape into the listening area. This type of design tries to capitalize on the back wave by manipulating it so that it reaches the listening area in phase with the front wave. Thus the overall sound is reinforced rather than degraded. This approach produces a more efficient speaker so that, all other things being equal, vented speakers can produce more volume per amplifier watt than acoustic suspension speakers.

Regardless of design, today's speakers far outdistance those of ten years ago in terms of quality of sound per dollar invested. Since no two speakers sound alike, regardless of design specifications, the ultimate concern when purchasing a speaker should probably not be design but how it sounds to the individual buyer.

Changing the Way We Look

Cosmetic surgery, once available only to the rich and famous, is a multimillion-dollar-a-year business in the United States. The rapid growth of this type of surgery has occurred even though patients must bear much of the cost, because most cosmetic surgery is not covered by insurance. The cost is considerable, ranging from $1,000 to more than $10,000, depending on the procedure, the doctor who does the surgery, and the geographical location in which the procedure is done. Some types of surgery are done on an outpatient basis, while others require several days in the hospital that add to the cost of the procedure.

Most cosmetic surgery is done to modify an individual's facial features. For removal of fine wrinkles around the mouth, brow, and eyes, dermabrasion is often chosen. Dermabrasion requires the physician to use skin planing tools to literally sand off the wrinkled areas after first injecting them with local anesthetic. Smoother skin results, but the patient has to wait about two weeks for the now pinkened skin to return to its normal color.

Another popular facial technique is skin peeling, or chemosurgery. In this procedure, a form of carbolic acid is applied to the face, the top layer of skin is burned off, and a scab results. About ten days later the scab comes off and there is a new, unblemished layer of skin that may take some weeks to return to its normal color. A proscription against direct exposure to the sun for about six months always accompanies this procedure. Fair-skinned individuals are the best candidates because other skin colors may develop irregular pigmentation as a result of this type of surgery.

Eyelid surgery, or blepharoplasty, is done when an individual has excessive skin on the upper lid or bags below the eye. To rid the individual of the "perpetually tired" look, incisions are made in the fold of the lid or just below the lower lash line. Excessive tissue is removed and the incision is stitched. This procedure is usually done on an outpatient basis, and the skin takes only two weeks to return to normal. Although complications are rare, there is always danger of hematomas (puffy areas filled with blood). Also, some people have excessive tearing and some have double vision because of muscle disturbances. Most of these problems either dissipate after several hours or are easily taken care of medically.

Probably the cosmetic surgery most people have heard of is the facelift. Over the past decade, new techniques have been developed so that facelifts can be performed on an outpatient basis. The procedure itself, using local anesthesia along with preoperative sedatives, involves incisions under the hairline and around the ears. Fatty tissue is removed, and the loose facial and neck skin is tightened. Sometimes eyelid surgery and chin augmentation accompany the facelift procedure. The recovery time varies from individual to individual but usually lasts several weeks.

Although not everyone is a good candidate for cosmetic surgery, several considerations are worth noting by individuals interested in changing the way they look. First, the choice of an experienced, highly recommended surgeon is a must. Besides plastic or reconstructive surgeons, specialists in dermatology or otolaryngology (ear, nose, and throat) who are board certified can perform cosmetic surgical procedures related to their field of specialization. A second consideration is your expectations: cosmetic surgery can't perform miracles. Although a facial change may be desired, the change you get may or may not meet your initial expectations, so discuss carefully with the doctor what will and won't occur as a result of the surgery. The last consideration is to weigh the expense against the hoped-for results. An old folk saying suggests "don't fix it if it ain't broke." It would seem that many people could save money and pain if they considered carefully whether a change in their looks is really warranted.

Fiber Optic Communications

One of the most important technological advances in recent years has been the advent of fiber optic communications. Whether it is used in an online computer system or an interactive television network, fiber optics is already a part of most Americans' lives. Because it will continue to replace much of what we use to communicate, it is important for people to understand as much as possible about fiber optic communications.

Fiber optic communications is simple: an electrical signal is converted to light, which is transmitted through an optical fiber, which is made of glass, to a distant receiver where it is converted back into the original electrical signal. The advantages of fiber optic communications over other transmission methods are substantial. A signal can be sent over longer distances without being boosted and without interference problems from nearby electrical fields. Additionally, its capacity is far greater than that of copper or coaxial cable systems, and the glass fiber itself is much lighter and smaller than the copper system. Notwithstanding these advantages, fiber optic communications are not problem free.

The most significant limitation in an optical communications system is the attentuation of the optical signal as it goes through the fiber. As information in the light is sent down the fiber, the light is attenuated (often called insertion lost) due to *Rayleigh scattering*. Rayleigh scattering refers to an effect created when a pulse of light is sent down a fiber and part of the pulse is blocked by dopants—microscopic particles in the glass—and scattered in all directions. Some of the light, 0.0001 percent, is scattered back in the opposite direction of the pulse; this is called the backscatter. Since dopants in optical fiber are uniformly distributed throughout the fiber due to the manufacturing process, this effect occurs along its entire length.

The Rayleigh scattering effect is similar to shining a flashlight in a fog at night. You can see fog because the particles of moisture reflect small amounts of light back at you: the light beam is diffused, or scattered, by the particles of moisture. A thick fog will scatter more of the light because there are more particles to obstruct it. The dopant particles in fiber act like the moisture particles of the fog, returning small amounts of light toward the source as the light hits them. Rayleigh scattering is the major loss factor in fiber optic communications.

Another cause of light loss in optical fiber is *Fresnel reflection*. Fresnel reflection is analogous to shining a flashlight at a window: most of the light passes through the window, but some of it reflects back. The angle at which the light beam hits the window determines whether or not the reflection will bounce back into the flashlight or into your eyes. Whenever light traveling through a material such as optical fiber encounters a material or different density, such as air, some of the light is reflected back toward the light source while the rest continues through the material. In optical fibers these sudden changes occur at the ends of fibers, at fiber breaks, and sometimes at splice joints. Obviously, fiber breaks are of great concern to fiber optic communications companies.

Since fiber optic systems are becoming more expansive and connected over longer distances, it is important to know how much light is lost in a regen, or length, of fiber. It is also important to be able to identify specific points on the fiber that have breaks or signal degradation. Although there are several methods to assess light loss, the most efficient means to pinpoint problems in a regen of fiber is the use of an *optical time domain reflectometer (OTDR)*. An OTDR is an electronic optical instrument that can be used to locate defects and faults and to determine the amount of signal loss at any point in an optical fiber by measuring backscatter levels and Fresnel reflection. The OTDR, unlike other methods, only needs access to one end of a fiber to make thousands of measurements along a fiber. The measurement data points can be between 0.5 and 16 meters apart. The selected data points are displayed on the OTDR screen as a line sloping down from left to right, with distance along the horizontal scale and signal level on the vertical scale. Using any two data points, the OTDR can reveal the distance and relative signal levels between them. Thus the OTDR can help companies that own fiber networks to repair breaks and prevent degradation of their signals: in short, to keep communications clear and repairs efficient.

EXAMINER'S
ASSESSMENT PROTOCOLS

LEVEL 10 ASSESSMENT PROTOCOLS

Stereo Speakers (605 words)

4:52

PART I: SILENT READING COMPREHENSION

Background Statement: "This selection is about stereo speakers. Read it to find out about the different types of speakers that people use to listen to music. Read it carefully because I am going to ask you to tell me what you know about stereo speakers based on the information in the passage." (*Note:* Be sure to time the student while reading so that you will be able to complete the Reading Fluency Chart in Part II.)

Teacher Directions: Once the student completes the silent reading, say, "Tell me about the passage you just read." Answers to the questions below that the student provides during the retelling should be marked "ua" in the appropriate blank to indicate that this response was unaided. Ask all remaining questions not addressed during the retelling and mark those the student answers with an "a" to indicate that the correct response was given after prompting by the teacher.

Questions/Answers	*Expository Grammar Element/ Level of Comprehension*
_____ 1. What causes sound to come out of a speaker? (*an electrical signal that is changed into sound waves*)	causation/literal
_____ 2. How are dynamic driver speakers and planar speakers different? (*planar speakers do not use a voice coil/magnet component*)	comparison/inferential
ua 3. Why is back wave a problem for makers of stereo speakers? (*if the speaker isn't designed to cope with back wave the back wave could cancel out the sound*)	causation/literal
a 4. Describe how acoustic suspension speakers eliminate back wave problems. (*they are designed to hold the back wave in the rear of the speaker's sealed enclosure*)	description/inferential
ua 5. How is a bass reflex speaker different from a sealed box speaker? (*bass reflex speakers are vented and produce more volume per watt*)	comparison/inferential
ua 6. Why would a bass reflex speaker be able to produce more volume per watt? (*because it uses the back wave to help produce the sound rather than cancelling the back wave*)	causation/inferential
ua 7. Why did the passage suggest that the final choice in buying a speaker should be how it sounds to the buyer rather than design type? (*because all modern speakers are well built but they sound different to different people, so people ought to buy the ones that sound best to them*)	problem resolution/evaluative
_____ 8. In terms of placement in a room, which type of dynamic driver speaker would be best to place against a wall? (*all things being equal, acoustic suspension speakers would work the best because the bass is vented and needs to be out from the wall*)	problem resolution/evaluative

ERROR TYPES | ERROR ANALYSIS

Stereo Speakers	mis-pronun.	sub-stitute	inser-tions	tchr. assist	omis-sions	Error Totals	Self-Correct.	(M) Meaning	(S) Syntax	(V) Visual
Almost everyone has listened										
to music at one time or										
another, yet few understand										
how stereo loudspeakers work.										
Simply put, all stereo										
loudspeakers are transducers										
that change electrical										
signals from an amplifier										
into sound waves. Beyond										
this simplistic explanation,										
stereo speakers diverge										
into many different types										
that even the most										
enthusiastic music lover										
can find perplexing.										
In general, all speakers										
can be placed into one of										
two major categories,										
depending on how the										
electrical signal is										
converted to sound.										
The most prevalent type										
of speaker uses *dynamic*										
drivers, those familiar cones										
and domes found in both										
low-cost and expensive										
models.//										
TOTALS										

Summary of Reading Behaviors (Strengths and Needs)

PART II: PERFORMANCE SUMMARY

Silent Reading Comprehension

_____ 0–1 questions missed = Easy

_____ 2 questions missed = Adequate

__✓__ 3+ questions missed = Too hard

Reading Fluency (WPM) *

_____ Above average fluency (210+ wpm)

_____ Average fluency (175–190 wpm)

_____ Below average fluency (less than 150 wpm)

*Words Per Minute (WPM) Calculation

Reading rate or _fluency_ is the estimate of how rapidly a student reads with accuracy. Calculate the student's reading fluency below using the words per minute (wpm) formula. Then compare his/her performance using the key provided.

Formula

Words in passage ÷ Time required for reading (minutes to nearest tenth) = WPM

Example:

760 (words) ÷ 3.2 (minutes) = 237 words per minute

Words in this passage = 605

Calculation for this student:

605 ÷ _____ = _____ WPM

Key:

Less than 150 WPM = Below average reading fluency

175–190 WPM = Average reading fluency

210+ WPM = Above average reading fluency

PART III: LISTENING COMPREHENSION

Directions: If you have decided not to continue to have the student read any other passages, then use this passage to begin assessing the student's listening comprehension (see page 19). Begin by reading the background statement for this passage and then say, "I am going to read this story to you. Please listen carefully because I will be asking you some questions after I finish reading it to you." After reading the passage, ask the student the questions associated with the passage. If the student correctly answers more than six questions, you will need to move to the next level and repeat the procedure.

Listening Comprehension

_____ 0–2 questions missed = move to the next passage level

_____ more than 2 questions missed = stop assessment or move down a level

Examiner's Notes:

LEVEL 11 ASSESSMENT PROTOCOLS

Changing the Way We Look (649 words)

PART I: SILENT READING COMPREHENSION

Background Statement: "This passage is about cosmetic surgery. Read it carefully and try to find out some facts about different cosmetic surgery techniques, because I am going to ask you to tell me as much as you can remember about the information in the passage." (*Note:* Be sure to time the student while reading so that you will be able to complete the Reading Fluency Chart in Part II.)

Teacher Directions: Once the student completes the silent reading, say, "Tell me about the passage you just read." Answers to the questions below that the student provides during the retelling should be marked "ua" in the appropriate blank to indicate that this response was unaided. Ask all remaining questions not addressed during the retelling and mark those the student answers with an "a" to indicate that the correct response was given after prompting by the teacher.

Questions/Answers	*Expository Grammar Element/ Level of Comprehension*
_____ 1. Describe what is done during dermabrasion. (*the surgeon uses a skin planing tool and scrapes off a layer of skin*)	description/inferential
_____ 2. What evidence did the passage provide that the number of cosmetic surgery procedures done per year is on the rise? (*it has become a multimillion-dollar business*)	comparison/inferential
_____ 3. How is chemosurgery different from dermabrasion? (*a chemical is used to burn off a layer of skin in chemosurgery while dermabrasion just sands away wrinkles; also chemosurgery results in a scab while dermabrasion does not*)	comparison/inferential
_____ 4. What are some of the possible complications associated with eyelid surgery? (*hematomas, excessive tearing, and double vision*)	description/literal
_____ 5. What are three considerations anyone considering cosmetic surgery should take into account before having it done? (*qualifications of the doctor, cost, and expectations*)	description/literal
_____ 6. What does the old folk saying suggest about cosmetic surgery? (*accept responses related to the idea that people should be satisfied with their looks rather than resort to surgery*)	problem resolution/evaluative
_____ 7. Besides plastic surgeons, what other kinds of doctors can perform some types of cosmetic surgery? (*dermatologists/skin doctors and otolaryngologists/ear, nose, and throat doctors*)	collection/literal
_____ 8. Why does eyelid surgery sometimes accompany a facelift? (*because if a person is having the facial skin tightened, it makes sense to get rid of fatty tissue around the eyes at the same time*)	collection/inferential

ERROR TYPES / ERROR ANALYSIS

Changing the Way We Look	mis-pronun.	sub-stitute	inser-tions	tchr. assist	omis-sions	Error Totals	Self-Correct.	(M) Meaning	(S) Syntax	(V) Visual
Cosmetic surgery, once										
available only to the rich										
and famous, is a multimillion-										
dollar-a-year business in										
the United States. The										
rapid growth of this										
type of surgery has										
occurred even though										
patients must bear much										
of the cost, because most										
cosmetic surgery is not										
covered by insurance. The										
cost is considerable,										
ranging from $1,000 to more than										
$10,000, depending on the										
procedure, the doctor who										
does the surgery, and the										
geographical location in										
which the procedure is done.										
Some types of surgery are										
done on an outpatient										
basis, while others require										
several days in the										
hospital that add to//										
the cost of the procedure.										
TOTALS										

Summary of Reading Behaviors (Strengths and Needs)

PART II: PERFORMANCE SUMMARY

Silent Reading Comprehension

_____ 0–1 questions missed = Easy

_____ 2 questions missed = Adequate

_____ 3+ questions missed = Too hard

Reading Fluency (WPM)*

_____ Above average fluency (210+ wpm)

_____ Average fluency (175–190 wpm)

_____ Below average fluency (less than 150 wpm)

*Words Per Minute (WPM) Calculation

Reading rate or *fluency* is the estimate of how rapidly a student reads with accuracy. Calculate the student's reading fluency below using the words per minute (wpm) formula. Then compare his/her performance using the key provided.

Formula
Words in passage ÷ Time required for reading (minutes to nearest tenth) = WPM

Example:
760 (words) ÷ 3.2 (minutes) = 237 words per minute

Words in this passage = 649

Calculation for this student:

649 ÷ _____ = _____ WPM

Key:
Less than 150 WPM = Below average reading fluency
175–190 WPM = Average reading fluency
210+ WPM = Above average reading fluency

PART III: LISTENING COMPREHENSION

Directions: If you have decided not to continue to have the student read any other passages, then use this passage to begin assessing the student's listening comprehension (see page 19). Begin by reading the background statement for this passage and then say, "I am going to read this story to you. Please listen carefully because I will be asking you some questions after I finish reading it to you." After reading the passage, ask the student the questions associated with the passage. If the student correctly answers more than six questions, you will need to move to the next level and repeat the procedure.

Listening Comprehension

_____ 0–2 questions missed = move to the next passage level

_____ more than 2 questions missed = stop assessment or move down a level

Examiner's Notes:

PART I: SILENT READING COMPREHENSION

Background Statement: "This selection is about fiber optic communications. Read the passage to discover some of the characteristics and problems associated with fiber optic communications. Read it carefully because I am going to ask you to tell me about the entire passage when you finish reading it." (*Note:* Be sure to time the student while reading so that you will be able to complete the Reading Fluency Chart in Part II.)

Teacher Directions: Once the student completes the silent reading, say, "Tell me about the passage you just read." Answers to the questions below that the student provides during the retelling should be marked "ua" in the appropriate blank to indicate that this response was unaided. Ask all remaining questions not addressed during the retelling and mark those the student answers with an "a" to indicate that the correct response was given after prompting by the teacher.

Questions/Answers	*Expository Grammar Element/ Level of Comprehension*
_____ 1. What two advantages does fiber optics have over other forms of communications transmission? (*no interference problems, does not need boosting over long distances, greater capacity, lighter and smaller*)	collection/literal
_____ 2. What are dopants? (*microscopic particles found in all optic fibers*)	description/literal
_____ 3. Why is loss of light in optic fiber a major concern of companies that use it for communication? (*poor signals or even a complete system shutdown*)	problem resolution/evaluative
_____ 4. What is Rayleigh scattering and why is it always present? (*the light that is reflected back toward its source due to dopants; because of the manufacturing process*)	causation/literal
_____ 5. Explain the main difference between Rayleigh scattering and Fresnel reflection. (*Rayleigh scattering caused by dopants, Fresnel reflection caused by fiber breaks, splices, or the end of fiber; accept plausible responses even if related to the fog versus light through glass analogy*)	comparison/inferential
_____ 6. How are a regen and an optical time domain reflectometer related? (*OTDR used to pinpoint light loss in any regen*)	collection/inferential
_____ 7. What separates the OTDR from other devices designed to pinpoint loss of light in fiber optic cable? (*only need access to one end of a fiber to make measurements*)	comparison/literal
_____ 8. Why would it be safe to say that OTDRs and other devices will be in greater demand in the future than they are now? (*because of the expansion of fiber optic communications*)	collection/evaluative

ERROR TYPES

	mis-pronun.	sub-stitute	inser-tions	tchr. assist	omis-sions	Error Totals	Self-Correct.	(M) Meaning	(S) Syntax	(V) Visual
Fiber Optic Communications										
One of the most important										
technological advances in										
recent years has been the										
advent of fiber optic										
communications. Whether it										
is used in an online										
computer system or an										
interactive television										
network, fiber optics is										
already a part of most										
Americans' lives. Because										
it will continue to replace										
much of what we use to										
communicate, it is										
important for people to										
understand as much as										
possible about fiber optic										
communications. Fiber										
optic commmunications is										
simple: an electrical										
signal is converted to										
light, which is transmitted										
through an optical fiber,										
which is made of glass,										
to a distant receiver										
where it// *is converted*										
back....										
TOTALS										

PART II: PERFORMANCE SUMMARY

Silent Reading Comprehension

_____ 0–1 questions missed = Easy

_____ 2 questions missed = Adequate

_____ 3+ questions missed = Too hard

Reading Fluency (WPM)*

_____ Above average fluency (210+ wpm)

_____ Average fluency (175–190 wpm)

_____ Below average fluency (less than 150 wpm)

*Words Per Minute (WPM) Calculation

Reading rate or *fluency* is the estimate of how rapidly a student reads with accuracy. Calculate the student's reading fluency below, using the words per minute (wpm) formula. Then compare his/her performance using the key provided.

Formula

Words in passage ÷ Time required for reading (minutes to nearest tenth) = WPM

Example:

760 (words) ÷ 3.2 (minutes) = 237 words per minute

Words in this passage = 760

Calculation for this student:

760 ÷ _____ = _____ WPM

Key:

Less than 150 WPM = Below average reading fluency

175–190 WPM = Average reading fluency

210+ WPM = Above average reading fluency

PART III: LISTENING COMPREHENSION

Directions: If you have decided not to continue to have the student read any other passages, then use this passage to begin assessing the student's listening comprehension (see page 19). Begin by reading the background statement for this passage and then say, "I am going to read this story to you. Please listen carefully because I will be asking you some questions after I finish reading it to you." After reading the passage, ask the student the questions associated with the passage.

Listening Comprehension

_____ 0–2 questions missed = move to the next passage level

_____ more than 2 questions missed = stop assessment or move down a level

Examiner's Notes:

APPENDIX

EXAMINER'S ASSESSMENT FORMS

- INTEREST/ATTITUDE INTERVIEW: PRIMARY FORM
- INTEREST/ATTITUDE INTERVIEW: UPPER LEVEL FORM
- MISCUE GRIDS
- MISCUE ANALYSIS SUMMARY
- FLUENCY (Words per Minute) CALCULATION: Grades 10–12
- STUDENT SUMMARY FORMS

Interest/Attitude Interview

PRIMARY FORM

Student's Name: _____ Age: _____

Date: _____ Examiner: _____

Introductory Statement: *[Student's name], before you read some stories for me, I would like to ask you some questions.*

Home Life

1. Where do you live? Do you know your address? What is it?

2. Who lives in your house with you?

3. What kinds of jobs do you have at home?

4. What is one thing that you really like to do at home?

5. Do you ever read at home? [*If yes, ask:*] When do you read and what was the last thing you read? [*If no, ask:*] Does anyone ever read to you? [*If so, ask:*] Who, and how often?

6. Do you have a bedtime on school nights? [*If no, ask:*] When do you go to bed?

7. Do you have a TV in your room? How much TV do you watch every day? What are your favorite shows?

8. What do you like to do with your friends?

9. Do you have any pets? Do you collect things? Do you take any kinds of lessons?

10. When you make a new friend, what is something that your friend ought to know about you?

School Life

1. Besides recess and lunch, what do you like about school?

2. Do you get to read much in school?

3. Are you a good reader or a not-so-good reader? [*If a good reader, ask:*] What makes a person a good reader? [*If a not-so-good reader, ask:*] What causes a person to not be a good reader?

4. If you could pick any book to read, what would the book be about?

5. Do you like to write? What kind of writing do you do in school? What is the favorite thing you have written about?

6. Who has helped you the most in school? How did that person help you?

7. Do you have a place at home to study?

8. Do you get help with your homework? Who helps you?

9. What was the last book you read for school?

10. If you were helping someone learn to read, what could you do to help that person?

Interest/Attitude Interview

UPPER LEVEL FORM

Student's Name: _____ Age: _____

Date: _____ Examiner: _____

Introductory Statement: *[Student's name], before you read some stories for me, I would like to ask you some questions.*

Home Life

1. How many people are there in your family?

2. Do you have your own room or do you share a room? [*Ask this only if it is apparent that the student has siblings.*]

3. Do your parent(s) work? What kinds of jobs do they have?

4. Do you have jobs around the house? What are they?

5. What do you usually do after school?

6. Do you have a TV in your room? How much time do you spend watching TV each day? What are your favorite shows?

7. Do you have a bedtime during the week? What time do you usually go to bed on a school night?

8. Do you get an allowance? How much?

9. Do you belong to any clubs at school or outside school? What are they?

10. What are some things that you really like to do? Do you collect things, have any hobbies, or take lessons outside school?

School Environment

1. Do you like school? What is your favorite class? Your least favorite class?

2. Do you have a special place to study at home?

3. How much homework do you have on a typical school night? Does anyone help you with your homework? Who?

4. Do you consider yourself a good reader or a not-so-good reader? [*If a good reader, ask:*] What has helped you most to become a good reader? [*If a not-so-good reader, ask:*] What causes someone to be a not-so-good reader?

5. If I gave you the choice of selecting a book about any topic, what would you choose to read about?

6. What is one thing you can think of that would help you become a better reader? Is there anything else?

7. Do you like to write? What kind of writing assignments do you like best?

8. If you went to a new school, what is one thing that you would want the teachers to know about you as a student?

9. If you were helping someone learn to read, what would be the most important thing you could do to help that person?

10. How will knowing how to read help you in the future?

	mis-pronun.	sub-stitute	inser-tions	tchr. assist	omis-sions	Error Totals	Self-Correct.	(M) Meaning	(S) Syntax	(V) Visual
ERROR TYPES						ERROR ANALYSIS				
TOTALS										

Summary of Reading Behaviors (Strengths and Needs)

MISCUE ANALYSIS

Directions: *Circle all reading behaviors you observed.*

A. Fundamental Behaviors Observed

L → R Directionality   1 to 1 Matching   Searching for Clues   Cross-Checking

B. Word Attack Behaviors

No Attempt   Mispronunciation (Invented word)   Substitutes

Skips/Reads On   Asks for Help   Repeats   Attempts to Self-Correct

"Sounds Out" (Segmenting)   Blends Sounds   Structural Analysis (Root words, Affixes)

C. Cueing Systems Used in Attempting Words

CUEING TOOL	MISCUE EXAMPLES	ACTUAL TEXT
(M) Meaning		
(S) Syntax		
(V) Visual		

D. Fluency (word by word → fluent reading)

Word by Word _____   Mixed Phrasing _____   Fluent Reading _____   Fluency Rate in Seconds _____

Performance Summary

Silent Reading Comprehension

_____ 0–1 question missed = Easy

_____ 2 questions missed = Adequate

_____ 3+ questions missed = Too hard

Oral Reading Accuracy

_____ 0–1 oral error = Easy

_____ 2–5 oral errors = Adequate

_____ 6+ oral errors = Too hard

Continue to the next reading passage? _____ Yes   _____ No

ERROR TYPES **ERROR ANALYSIS**

	mis-pronun.	sub-stitute	inser-tions	tchr. assist	omis-sions	Error Totals	Self-Correct.	(M) Meaning	(S) Syntax	(V) Visual
TOTALS										

Summary of Reading Behaviors (Strengths and Needs)

MISCUE ANALYSIS

Directions: *Circle all reading behaviors you observed.*

A. Fundamental Behaviors Observed

L → R Directionality   1 to 1 Matching   Searching for Clues   Cross-Checking

B. Word Attack Behaviors

No Attempt   Mispronunciation (Invented word)   Substitutes

Skips/Reads On   Asks for Help   Repeats   Attempts to Self-Correct

"Sounds Out" (Segmenting)   Blends Sounds   Structural Analysis (Root words, Affixes)

C. Cueing Systems Used in Attempting Words

CUEING TOOL	MISCUE EXAMPLES	ACTUAL TEXT
(M) Meaning		
(S) Syntax		
(V) Visual		

D. Fluency (word by word → fluent reading)

Word by Word _____   Mixed Phrasing _____   Fluent Reading _____   Fluency Rate in Seconds _____

Performance Summary

Silent Reading Comprehension

_____ 0–1 question missed = Easy

_____ 2 questions missed = Adequate

_____ 3+ questions missed = Too hard

Oral Reading Accuracy

_____ 0–1 oral error = Easy

_____ 2–5 oral errors = Adequate

_____ 6+ oral errors = Too hard

Continue to the next reading passage? _____ Yes   _____ No

mis-pronun.	sub-stitute	inser-tions	tchr. assist	omis-sions	Error Totals	Self-Correct.	(M) Meaning	(S) Syntax	(V) Visual
TOTALS									

ERROR TYPES

ERROR ANALYSIS

Summary of Reading Behaviors (Strengths and Needs)

MISCUE ANALYSIS

Directions: *Circle all reading behaviors you observed.*

A. Fundamental Behaviors Observed

L → R Directionality   1 to 1 Matching   Searching for Clues   Cross-Checking

B. Word Attack Behaviors

No Attempt   Mispronunciation (Invented word)   Substitutes

Skips/Reads On   Asks for Help   Repeats   Attempts to Self-Correct

"Sounds Out" (Segmenting)   Blends Sounds   Structural Analysis (Root words, Affixes)

C. Cueing Systems Used in Attempting Words

CUEING TOOL	MISCUE EXAMPLES	ACTUAL TEXT
(M) Meaning		
(S) Syntax		
(V) Visual		

D. Fluency (word by word → fluent reading)

Word by Word _____   Mixed Phrasing _____   Fluent Reading _____   Fluency Rate in Seconds _____

Performance Summary

Silent Reading Comprehension

_____ 0–1 question missed = Easy

_____ 2 questions missed = Adequate

_____ 3+ questions missed = Too hard

Oral Reading Accuracy

_____ 0–1 oral error = Easy

_____ 2–5 oral errors = Adequate

_____ 6+ oral errors = Too hard

Continue to the next reading passage? _____ Yes   _____ No

ERROR ANALYSIS

(M) Meaning	(S) Syntax	(V) Visual

Self-Correct.

Error Totals

ERROR TYPES

mis-pronun.	sub-stitute	inser-tions	tchr. assist	omis-sions

TOTALS

Summary of Reading Behaviors (Strengths and Needs)

MISCUE ANALYSIS

Directions: *Circle all reading behaviors you observed.*

A. Fundamental Behaviors Observed

L → R Directionality   1 to 1 Matching   Searching for Clues   Cross-Checking

B. Word Attack Behaviors

No Attempt   Mispronunciation (Invented word)   Substitutes

Skips/Reads On   Asks for Help   Repeats   Attempts to Self-Correct

"Sounds Out" (Segmenting)   Blends Sounds   Structural Analysis (Root words, Affixes)

C. Cueing Systems Used in Attempting Words

CUEING TOOL	MISCUE EXAMPLES	ACTUAL TEXT
(M) Meaning		
(S) Syntax		
(V) Visual		

D. Fluency (word by word → fluent reading)

Word by Word _____   Mixed Phrasing _____   Fluent Reading _____   Fluency Rate in Seconds _____

Performance Summary

Silent Reading Comprehension

_____ 0–1 question missed = Easy

_____ 2 questions missed = Adequate

_____ 3+ questions missed = Too hard

Oral Reading Accuracy

_____ 0–1 oral error = Easy

_____ 2–5 oral errors = Adequate

_____ 6+ oral errors = Too hard

Continue to the next reading passage? _____ Yes   _____ No

ERROR ANALYSIS

(M) Meaning	(S) Syntax	(V) Visual

ERROR TYPES

mis-pronun.	sub-stitute	inser-tions	tchr. assist	omis-sions	Error Totals	Self-Correct.

TOTALS

Summary of Reading Behaviors (Strengths and Needs)

MISCUE ANALYSIS

Directions: *Circle all reading behaviors you observed.*

A. Fundamental Behaviors Observed

L → R Directionality   1 to 1 Matching   Searching for Clues   Cross-Checking

B. Word Attack Behaviors

No Attempt   Mispronunciation (Invented word)   Substitutes

Skips/Reads On   Asks for Help   Repeats   Attempts to Self-Correct

"Sounds Out" (Segmenting)   Blends Sounds   Structural Analysis (Root words, Affixes)

C. Cueing Systems Used in Attempting Words

CUEING TOOL	MISCUE EXAMPLES	ACTUAL TEXT
(M) Meaning		
(S) Syntax		
(V) Visual		

D. Fluency (word by word → fluent reading)

Word by Word _____   Mixed Phrasing _____   Fluent Reading _____   Fluency Rate in Seconds _____

Performance Summary

Silent Reading Comprehension

_____ 0–1 question missed = Easy

_____ 2 questions missed = Adequate

_____ 3+ questions missed = Too hard

Oral Reading Accuracy

_____ 0–1 oral error = Easy

_____ 2–5 oral errors = Adequate

_____ 6+ oral errors = Too hard

Continue to the next reading passage? _____ Yes   _____ No

	ERROR TYPES						Error Totals	Self-Correct.	ERROR ANALYSIS		
	mis-pronun.	sub-stitute	inser-tions	tchr. assist	omis-sions				(M) Meaning	(S) Syntax	(V) Visual
TOTALS											

Summary of Reading Behaviors (Strengths and Needs)

MISCUE ANALYSIS

Directions: *Circle all reading behaviors you observed.*

A. Fundamental Behaviors Observed

L → R Directionality   1 to 1 Matching   Searching for Clues   Cross-Checking

B. Word Attack Behaviors

No Attempt   Mispronunciation (Invented word)   Substitutes

Skips/Reads On   Asks for Help   Repeats   Attempts to Self-Correct

"Sounds Out" (Segmenting)   Blends Sounds   Structural Analysis (Root words, Affixes)

C. Cueing Systems Used in Attempting Words

CUEING TOOL	MISCUE EXAMPLES	ACTUAL TEXT
(M) Meaning		
(S) Syntax		
(V) Visual		

D. Fluency (word by word → fluent reading)

Word by Word _____   Mixed Phrasing _____   Fluent Reading _____   Fluency Rate in Seconds _____

Performance Summary

Silent Reading Comprehension

_____ 0–1 question missed = Easy

_____ 2 questions missed = Adequate

_____ 3+ questions missed = Too hard

Oral Reading Accuracy

_____ 0–1 oral error = Easy

_____ 2–5 oral errors = Adequate

_____ 6+ oral errors = Too hard

Continue to the next reading passage? _____ Yes   _____ No

WORDS PER MINUTE (WPM) CALCULATION: GRADES 10–12

Reading rate or *fluency* is the estimate of how rapidly a student reads with accuracy. A student's reading fluency slows somewhat when reading expository or nonfiction texts (as compared to fiction or narrative texts). Calculate the student's reading fluency below, using the words per minute (WPM) formula. Then compare his/her performance using the key provided.

Formula
Words in passage ÷ Time required for reading (minutes to nearest tenth) = WPM

Example:
760 (words) ÷ 3.2 (minutes) = 237 words per minute

Key:
Less than 150 WPM = Below average reading fluency
175–190 WPM = Average reading fluency
210+ WPM = Above average reading fluency

STUDENT SUMMARY

Student's Name _____

Examiner _____

Form(s) Used   A   B   C   D   E

I. Performance on Sentences for Passage Selection

_____ Highest level with zero (0) errors

_____ First level with two (2) or more errors

II. Overall Performance Levels on Reading Passages

	Narrative Passages (A, B)	*Expository (Nonfiction) Passages (C, D, E)*
Easy (Independent)	_____	_____
Adequate (Instructional)	_____	_____
Too Hard (Frustration)	_____	_____
Average Reading Fluency Rate	_____	_____

III. Miscue Summary Chart

Directions: *Enter total number of miscues from ALL passages into each block indicated.*

	Mispronunciation	Substitutions	Insertions	Teacher Assists	Omissions
Total Miscues from All Passages					

(Purpose: To identify patterns of miscues based on highest frequency of errors to inform instructional decisions.)

IV. Error Analyses (Cueing Systems)

Directions: *Enter total number of times (all passages) the student used each of the cueing systems when* *miscue was made.*

(Purpose: To determine the extent to which cueing systems are used to identify unknown words in print.

Meaning Cues (M) _____

Syntax Cues (S) _____

Visual Cues (V) _____

V. Other Observations

VI. Instructional Implications

STUDENT SUMMARY

Student's Name _____

Examiner _____

Form(s) Used   A   B   C   D   E

I. Performance on Sentences for Passage Selection

_____   Highest level with zero (0) errors

_____   First level with two (2) or more errors

II. Overall Performance Levels on Reading Passages

	Narrative Passages (A, B)	*Expository (Nonfiction) Passages (C, D, E)*
Easy (Independent)	_____	_____
Adequate (Instructional)	_____	_____
Too Hard (Frustration)	_____	_____
Average Reading Fluency Rate	_____	_____

III. Miscue Summary Chart

Directions: *Enter total number of miscues from ALL passages into each block indicated.*

	Mispronunciation	Substitutions	Insertions	Teacher Assists	Omissions
Total Miscues from All Passages					

(Purpose: To identify patterns of miscues based on highest frequency of errors to inform instructional decisions.)

IV. Error Analyses (Cueing Systems)

Directions: *Enter total number of times (all passages) the student used each of the cueing systems when a miscue was made.*

(Purpose: To determine the extent to which cueing systems are used to identify unknown words in print.)

Meaning Cues (M)   _____

Syntax Cues (S)   _____

Visual Cues (V)   _____

V. Other Observations

VI. Instructional Implications

Student's Name _____

Examiner _____

Form(s) Used   A   B   C   D   E

I. Performance on Sentences for Passage Selection

_____ Highest level with zero (0) errors

_____ First level with two (2) or more errors

II. Overall Performance Levels on Reading Passages

	Narrative Passages (A, B)	Expository (Nonfiction) Passages (C, D, E)
Easy (Independent)	_____	_____
Adequate (Instructional)	_____	_____
Too Hard (Frustration)	_____	_____
Average Reading Fluency Rate	_____	_____

III. Miscue Summary Chart

Directions: *Enter total number of miscues from ALL passages into each block indicated.*

	Mispronunciation	Substitutions	Insertions	Teacher Assists	Omissions
Total Miscues from All Passages					

(Purpose: To identify patterns of miscues based on highest frequency of errors to inform instructional decisions.)

IV. Error Analyses (Cueing Systems)

Directions: *Enter total number of times (all passages) the student used each of the cueing systems when a miscue was made.*

(Purpose: To determine the extent to which cueing systems are used to identify unknown words in print.)

Meaning Cues (M) _____

Syntax Cues (S) _____

Visual Cues (V) _____

V. Other Observations

VI. Instructional Implications

STUDENT SUMMARY

Student's Name _____

Examiner _____

Form(s) Used   A   B   C   D   E

I. Performance on Sentences for Passage Selection

_____   Highest level with zero (0) errors

_____   First level with two (2) or more errors

II. Overall Performance Levels on Reading Passages

	Narrative Passages (A, B)	Expository (Nonfiction) Passages (C, D, E)
Easy (Independent)	_____	_____
Adequate (Instructional)	_____	_____
Too Hard (Frustration)	_____	_____
Average Reading Fluency Rate	_____	_____

III. Miscue Summary Chart

Directions: *Enter total number of miscues from ALL passages into each block indicated.*

	Mispronunciation	Substitutions	Insertions	Teacher Assists	Omissions
Total Miscues from All Passages					

Purpose: To identify patterns of miscues based on highest frequency of errors to inform instructional decisions.)

IV. Error Analyses (Cueing Systems)

Directions: *Enter total number of times (all passages) the student used each of the cueing systems when a miscue was made.*

(Purpose: To determine the extent to which cueing systems are used to identify unknown words in print.)

Meaning Cues (M)   _____

Syntax Cues (S)   _____

Visual Cues (V)   _____

V. Other Observations

VI. Instructional Implications

▰▰▰▰▰▰▰▰▰▰▰▰▰▰▰▰▰▰▰▰▰▰▰▰▰

STUDENT SUMMARY
▪ ▪

Student's Name _____

Examiner _____

Form(s) Used   A   B   C   D   E

. Performance on Sentences for Passage Selection

_____ Highest level with zero (0) errors

_____ First level with two (2) or more errors

I. Overall Performance Levels on Reading Passages

	Narrative Passages (A, B)	Expository (Nonfiction) Passages (C, D, E)
Easy (Independent)	_____	_____
Adequate (Instructional)	_____	_____
Too Hard (Frustration)	_____	_____
Average Reading Fluency Rate	_____	_____

II. Miscue Summary Chart

Directions: *Enter total number of miscues from ALL passages into each block indicated.*

	Mispronunciation	Substitutions	Insertions	Teacher Assists	Omissions
Total Miscues from All Passages					

(Purpose: To identify patterns of miscues based on highest frequency of errors to inform instructional decisions.)

IV. Error Analyses (Cueing Systems)

Directions: *Enter total number of times (all passages) the student used each of the cueing systems when a miscue was made.*

(Purpose: To determine the extent to which cueing systems are used to identify unknown words in print.)

Meaning Cues (M)   _____

Syntax Cues (S)   _____

Visual Cues (V)   _____

V. Other Observations

VI. Instructional Implications